I0072389

"*The Business Immunity System* is indispensable reading that must be implemented into any enterprise that cares about its employees and its future… Rachid has laid out very vital principles to ensure any company has the needed defenses against hidden crime and destructive influences. You can call him "the corporate doctor."

Joe Yazbeck

founder and president of Prestige Leadership Advisors and author of the best selling book, No Fear Speaking

"There is a new breed of digital criminals out there that are focused on accessing our personal and business information to make a profit. *The Business Immunity System* identifies the problems and provides practical solutions to protect yourself, your employees, and your business information. The solutions in this book need to be implemented immediately!"

Bill Lenahan

CEO of OffSite Vision Holding Inc.

"In an ever-changing landscape of rules and regulations, *The Business Immunity System* grasps the timeless principles that allow for responsible screening and due diligence policies and procedures. Every entrepreneur or professional who is responsible for hiring and talent selection can't afford to remain ignorant of these background checking concepts."

Nick Friedman

co-founder and president of College Hunks Hauling Junk Franchises

"Rarely is such a practical and insightful guide available to business owners. As an employment-law attorney dealing with HR and "privacy" issues on a daily basis, I highly recommend *The Business Immunity System*. It is an extremely useful tool for companies and business owners who are attempting to navigate the murky waters of its duty to provide a safe workplace vs. its duty to avoid violations of privacy rights. Rachid, with many years of hands-on experience, helps the reader address those issues while avoiding legal complications."

Claire Saady

attorney and partner at SAADY & SAXE, P.A

"Rachid has written a book we all need in our complicated, high-risk business world. Running a business is hard enough and we often take risks because we don't know what we don't know! Rather than learn the hard way, Rachid has made it easier for us to think more strategically with a proven system to enable business owners to be proactive in our decision making around hiring talent and protecting our world. He helps us consider the various risks and benefits in each situation with real life examples that we can relate to. As CEO of a strengths-based leadership and team development organization, I strongly believe that business leaders should focus on what they are BEST at. Rachid has done that in data handling, privacy, and background checks. Rachid's expertise comes to us in an easy-to-read and practical guide to support our business success, freeing the rest of us up to enjoy the reasons why we started our business in the first place and to focus our own strengths."

Jayne Jenkins

CEO of Churchill Leadership Group Inc.
Executive Leadership and Strengths Coach: ACTP/PCP ICF

"Security is of prime importance to organizations and individuals, whether it is about hiring people or about safeguarding personal data or vital information. This growing social and personal issue is addressed In *The Business Immunity System*. Rachid Zahidi does a great job of outlining all the possible pitfalls for both organizations and individuals, and advising them about precautions that they need to take to avoid these. A must read for everyone!"

Nooruddin (Rudy) Karsan
co-founder and former CEO of Kenexa Corp and co-author of
We: How to Increase Performance and Profits through Full Engagement

"If only a business could make itself completely immune! Of course, while this is not possible, Rachid's book is a great guide to data protection, privacy and the all-important pre-employment background check. This is a quick read, in lay terms, and gives employers what they need to know to protect themselves from easily-preventable mistakes."

Bruce Berg
founder of Berg Consulting Group

"Rachid candidly offers sobering insight on the costs of failing to recognize and act on the fact that professionally performed background checks of prospective employees are no longer discretionary budgeting issues. It's a form of preemptive catastrophic insurance and is mandatory for any business wanting to stay in business. In an economy in which technology is increasingly displacing human labor, those competing for jobs are compelled to both enhance their positive attributes and obfuscate the negative. In such an environment "trust, but verify" is not just an operational necessity but an existential one. *The Business Immunity System* provides the starting point."

Roger Arnold
chief economist for ALM Advisors LLC and columnist for TheStreet

"*The Business Immunity System* provides an outstanding insider's perspective for businesses to learn proven techniques and implement procedures that safeguard corporate data—it's a how to manual on the right way to use background checks to improve hiring decisions. Rachid has created an invaluable resource for anyone responsible for data security or screening new hires."

Joe Ambrefe
founder and CEO of SecurityPoint Media

"This must-read book highlights the main principles of responsible background checks. It stands out with its balanced approach to the necessity of a good business system that protects both business owners and consumers from regulations and law violations. It will help you inoculate against defects and ailments that can jeopardize the health and longevity of your business."

John C. Marshall, Ph.D
president of Self Management Group

"Rachid's book is a must read for any leader, business owner, or head of HR that wants to hire the right talent. One of the biggest mistakes that I see companies trip up on is to make hiring decisions on little or incorrect data. This book is unique in that it shows you the inside world of background checks and how despite your best efforts, you can get false information."

Mary Key, Ph.D.
executive coach, speaker, author, and president of Key Associates, Inc.

"While the target of this book is clearly businesses with the goal to help them strengthen their 'Business Immunity System' there are also very important messages for consumers to learn about protecting their privacy and information. Generations ago many people did not lock their doors because they felt safe. Today people are learning that the doors to their data must be well protected or there can be dire consequences. In a time of ubiquitous information gathering, Rachid does a superb job of educating business owners, management professionals, and consumers about the evolving social views of privacy and how to avoid many of the pitfalls that are inherent in a society that consumes massive amounts of information."

W. Barry Nixon, SPHR

COO of PreemploymentDirectory.com and publisher of the Annual Background Screening Industry Buyers Resource Guide *and* The Background Buzz

"Employer use of criminal records is becoming more complex and Rachid examines the issue with evenhanded experience."

Derek Hinton

author and president of CRAzoom and CrimApollo

THE

BUSINESS

IMMUNITY

SYSTEM

THE

BUSINESS

IMMUNITY

SYSTEM

The Pitfalls & Side Effects of

Data Handling, Privacy Issues,

& Background Checks

RACHID ZAHIDI

Advantage®

Published by Advantage, Charleston, South Carolina.
Member of Advantage Media Group.

ADVANTAGE is a registered trademark and the Advantage colophon is a trademark of Advantage Media Group, Inc.

Printed in the United States of America.

ISBN: 978-159932-539-2
LCCN: 2015931570

Book design by George Stevens.

This publication is designed to provide accurate and authoritative information in regard to the subject matter covered. It is sold with the understanding that the publisher is not engaged in rendering legal, accounting, or other professional services. If legal advice or other expert assistance is required, the services of a competent professional person should be sought.

Advantage Media Group is proud to be a part of the Tree Neutral® program. Tree Neutral offsets the number of trees consumed in the production and printing of this book by taking proactive steps such as planting trees in direct proportion to the number of trees used to print books. To learn more about Tree Neutral, please visit www.treeneutral.com. To learn more about Advantage's commitment to being a responsible steward of the environment, please visit www.advantagefamily.com/green

Advantage Media Group is a publisher of business, self-improvement, and professional development books and online learning. We help entrepreneurs, business leaders, and professionals share their Stories, Passion, and Knowledge to help others Learn & Grow. Do you have a manuscript or book idea that you would like us to consider for publishing? Please visit advantagefamily.com or call 1.866.775.1696.

TABLE OF CONTENTS

INTRODUCTION

How do thieves embezzle tens of thousands of dollars without breaking a lock? It happens when you, as a business owner or hiring manager, let them into your workplace and put them in the ideal position to steal from you.

Recently, I met a business owner who invested all of her savings, heart, and soul into her business, but she was naïve. She met a job candidate who interviewed well. Everything was good on paper and in person. This individual charmed the owner, and she hired her. The new hire was responsible for receivables and oversaw some of the finances. Everything was going well until a few months later, when the new hire didn't show up for work. The owner was worried, so she called her new employee but couldn't get in touch. Finally, she contacted the authorities, and they obtained the missing woman's personal information. Police in a difference state wanted the individual for stealing money from a company where she had previously worked. In a panic, the business owner reviewed her own company's financial records and saw that about

$75,000 was missing. Law enforcement reported the thief was already in a different jurisdiction, and they were unable to locate her. The woman's business took a financial hit.

Theft like that can destroy a business. In fact, according to the US Department of Commerce, 30 percent of small business failure is caused by employee theft.

As the owner and CEO of Sentinel Background Checks, I often encounter stories of businesses and business owners who have been victims of scams, theft, wrongful suits, and many other perils.

Think about your own business for a moment:

- What if you unknowingly hire a violent offender who rapes or assaults one of your employees?

- What if you turned away a potentially great employee because she seemed to have a criminal record, but that record was a mistake? What if she found out, sued you, and won?

- What if she found others you had turned away for the same mistaken reason, and they got together for a class-action lawsuit?

- What if you were found in violation of Equal Employment Opportunity Commission (EEOC) rules and regulations or the Fair Credit Reporting Act (FCRA)?

Any one of these scenarios can carry devastating consequences—and claiming ignorance in court is not a defense.

That's why I have written this book, which focuses on the main principles, pitfalls, and disasters of what, when, who, and why you (and anyone you entrust with this responsibility) must do background checks properly, responsibly, and ethically.

By following the principles of the proprietary Business Immunity System described in this book, you can improve the quality of your employees, simplify your procedures, and strengthen the systems that are ultimately responsible for the health and longevity of your business.

PRIVACY AND BACKGROUND CHECKS

Background checks are a contentious topic, raising questions that go to the heart of privacy, equal opportunity, and fair treatment. Some companies don't do background checks, they do them wrong, or they overdo them, which is usually the source of any problems that may emerge.

If you're using overly invasive, unjustified searches for the type of job you are looking to fill, you're likely violating laws and regulations related to the FCRA, the EEOC, and many others, depending on your industry.

On the other hand, if you are not doing background checks, you may be opening yourself up to lawsuits for negligent hiring. Lack of background checking can put many at risk of violence and abuse, including employees, customers, seniors, and kids. You are playing Russian roulette with your livelihood and the livelihood of others!

For instance, there is a case in which parents sued a school in New Hampshire because the school had hired an ex-convict. Had the school staff done a background check, they would have realized he had a criminal record. But they didn't, and he assaulted one of the kids. The parents filed a lawsuit in the US District Court of New Hampshire, and the offender was sentenced in November 2013 to three to eight years in state prison for convictions on charges of sexual assault and indecent exposure. This person already had a police record and was discharged from a previous school in a different state for a similar offense. He simply went to another state and got the same type of job again.

If you are already conducting background checks, congratulations. You are taking a step in the right direction—but hold on a minute! Are you compliant with laws and regulations governing the performance of background checks, and do your processes discriminate without you realizing it? Are you aware of the potential pitfalls? In 2013 a class-action lawsuit alleged Domino's Pizza was not providing copies of their reports to job applicants who had been turned down and was not separating the consent form from the application for employment. One of the job applicants caught on to that and found others who had also had the same experience. A group action suit ensued, ending when Domino's had to pay $2.5 million to a settlement fund.

There are people who argue for stronger background check legislation, while others say checks are discriminatory. The thing to remember is that all background checks must be justified. For a driving job, for example, if the applicant is responsible for transporting people, requesting the applicant's driving record or motor vehicle report is justified. You don't want someone with a history of reckless driving or driving under the influence of alcohol. If you're hiring for the medical field, you want to make sure that licenses are valid, verified, and no sanctions or penalties have been issued against the job applicants in a different state. You also need to do drug screening, because you don't want people under the influence of drugs to be responsible for injecting medications. They could inject patients with the wrong medication, mismatch prescriptions, provide an incorrect dosage, or inject themselves with the medication to get high!

In most cases, even if you go to court, you have to be able to show that your hiring practices are not way out of line or discriminatory. Background checks must be professional and relevant to the essential requirements of the job. Employers should be aware of their placement of disclaimers, waivers, and how they compose authorization forms. They should not bury important information in the text. They should be specific about how they'll carry out the check and what products they'll use. They should make sure they get a valid signature from applicants who understand clearly what they are signing, and they should give applicants an opportunity to dispute the background check results. By ensuring that practices are fair and nondiscriminatory and that paperwork is up to date, employers greatly reduce the risk of being sued and losing the lawsuit.

THE BENEFIT OF BACKGROUND CHECKS

The benefits of using a reputable background check provider are enormous. Businesses that have not conducted background checks in the past will get a new, headache-free screening process to build a better functioning team. Business owners and managers who have worked with less-than-reputable providers who are less concerned about compliance and more interested in cutting corners can benefit from better efficiency, personable customer service, and being treated with respect.

For many employers, keeping up with the rules, regulations, and best practices of background checking can be aggravating and confusing. That's why it is important to choose the right specialists and professionals, whose primary reason for existence is to be competent, reliable, communicative, and efficient with this important prerequisite to a safe hire.

Any good background check company should be able to educate you about these issues if you are not aware of them already. If you're using a background check company, you always want to verify it is professional in its operation, and there are important questions to ask, which we will discuss in this book. The replies will prove whether or not the company is keeping its information up to date. If you're relying heavily on such a company, be sure, as they say in the industry, to "trust but verify."

If you're using a background check company, you always want to verify it is professional in its operation, and there are important questions to ask, which we will discuss in this book.

A good background check should start with a Social Security (SS) trace, which reveals whether the job applicant has used aliases and where that person has lived. For jurisdictional reasons, your research on possible aliases must be done in the counties where your applicant has lived.

If you really want to get up-to-date information that is compliant with regulations, you have to go to the source. Often, that means the court itself, because that is where the most recent information is held. In databases that have been compiling information for years or decades there may be mistakes and mismatches. For example, cases or convictions can be attributed to the wrong person, or the information may be outdated. A good example is a case that has been expunged. You're not supposed to use such a case, according to the FCRA. However, if such a case circulates in an outdated database, and you're relying on that database alone, you may end up using it by accident. That's a mistake that will leave you vulnerable to a liability suit. You are responsible for vetting this information, verifying it, and examining all the different identifiers to confirm its validity.

To make the process even more complex, certain states have their own consumer protection laws, some of which were passed before the FCRA was enacted. Check to make sure there are no additional or different forms required by your individual state or regulations you must abide by when turning reports over to applicants. Some state laws require you to give the job applicant the report at the same time that you receive your copy. Some states even reduce the time frame during which convictions may be reported to as little as five years. When you receive a report, the person whose data was gathered also receives a report—always.

As is customary in the background checking industry, Sentinel Background Checks reports on data. We serve employers, property managers, and landlords. We also serve other background check companies, mostly to retrieve court data. That's usually done for criminal cases and criminal research at the court level, whether it's county, state, or federal courts. Our work involves extracting data directly from the source or retrieving copies of dockets and documents and helping to interpret that information.

The consumer reporting agencies that we supply with court data are savvy and compliant and share our commitment to the fair, responsible, and ethical practice of our profession. We work with a variety of qualified, vetted, and heavily tested suppliers for drug screening test results, motor vehicle records, credit reports, and so on, in international and other areas that are outside the coverage of our direct access to courts.

As CEO of Sentinel Background Checks, I have heard and seen the extremes, from business owners thinking a background check is a Google search to people pulling all kinds of reports without being aware of, or choosing to ignore, their obligations when it comes to securing consent, using the correct forms, and being aware of disclosure requirements or adverse action notification. I have seen large companies do background checks with providers who conducted searches for them and never secured a single consent form! We show our clients the specific rules and regulations of the FCRA and how easy it is to follow the compliance process. We supply most of the forms and provide ongoing updates and support.

Background check procedures are a necessity, not a luxury. It is never too late to start implementing an appropriate and compliant screening policy. We have clients who sobered up to this and found they were not using the right supplier. We have employers whose motivation to do background checks was prompted by a probation officer who showed up at their workplace to check on an employee they never knew had a criminal record.

People, information, and data are the heart of the issues surrounding background checks. This book contains a great deal of useful information to help you become more aware and responsible about how you use data and information for training, reference, or general awareness, as well as to better protect you as a consumer and business owner. If you want your business to operate like a well-oiled machine and not break down, you start by not putting defective parts in the machine!

At the end of the day, the onus is on us, as business owners and as consumers, to make sure we safeguard and monitor our information. The primary way to protect ourselves and our business is understanding how data can be used in safe, responsible, and respectful ways. By learning the facts about data collection and access, we can safeguard our most private accounts, our personal lives, and our livelihoods.

CHAPTER 1

A Generation without Privacy

How do we balance our curiosity and interest in information with our desire to keep our own data and attributes
private and safeguarded? It used to be more about physical
privacy and choosing what to do behind closed doors or
in public. Now the lines are getting blurred between physical and
digital privacy.

In the early years of the Internet, people were so excited about
the array of new opportunities and accessibility of data that they
were not thinking critically. There have been some more recent
cases, however, that have brought awareness to the dangers of not
being vigilant. Examples include the Craigslist killer and the New
Hampshire case of Amy Boyer whose stalker turned killer bought
her SS and location information online in order to track her down
and shot her as she was getting ready to leave work on October
15, 1999.[1]

After a few of these cases received publicity, people started
sobering up. Even social media giants, such as Facebook and

---

[1] | Moya, Alberto, "An Online Tragedy," *CBS News*, March 23, 2000,
http://www.cbsnews.com/news/an-online-tragedy/

Google, have been subject to the scrutiny of media and privacy rights groups, with big uproars over their privacy settings and how they are not upfront about their information gathering and distribution. Social networks generally prefer a default setting that discloses more rather than minimal information, and users must decide for themselves how much they'd like to share.

SOCIAL MEDIA AND PRIVACY

Users are starting to understand that they have to look at privacy settings more closely. They have to be careful to understand what they're getting into and with whom they're sharing information. Unfortunately, it's not until something really bad happens that people start paying more attention. The danger has to hit close to home, or some triggering event has to happen, something that makes the risk real, showing you how bad it can get if you don't pay attention.

Check all your privacy settings for social media. Don't disclose more than you need to. When it's of no consequence, do you really need to give out your real date of birth? Once you have reached a point where the negative side effects of using certain social media or websites outweigh the positives, you're probably going to stop using them. Sometimes, you can realize this when your information shows up in websites open to the general public or is shared with people you didn't intend it to be shared with. The commercial marketplace has a way of evening itself out. Once people stop participating in, or buying, certain products, services, or events, those entities eventually cease to exist. This requires the media, services, or websites—if they want to stay in business—to begin addressing people's concerns as a preventative measure.

If you have personal information on social media, you must be very aware of the potential consequences. Most social media searches are performed without malicious intent, but they do present the opportunity to spy and pry. Responsible employers who engage in social media searches typically seek posts or photos that indicate a tendency for violence or a history of racist comments. Generic comments, links to news stories, or pictures from your family vacation do not interest them.

Do a social media search on yourself, and see what comes up. You may want to consider keeping your personal pages separate from your professional networking pages.

There is no such thing as 100 percent anymore. You can only minimize the risks by being vigilant and not signing up for services you don't need. There are, obviously, people who take it to the extreme. There are people who don't have a profile on Facebook, Twitter, or LinkedIn. They barely use the Internet and may have one e-mail address or none at all. That's the extreme. But almost everyone now interacts in some way with the Internet, including banking and/or shopping online.

The use of social media is similar to locking or not locking doors. Generations ago, in a lot of places, people didn't lock their doors, and some were attacked or killed as a result. So, people started locking their doors. Securing your information is basic safety; it's like locking your door when you leave for work in the morning or locking it behind you when you get home at night.

One of my favorite quotations comes from Jim Rohn: "Discipline weighs in ounces, but regret weighs in tons." We all need a little bit of discipline to keep ourselves free of regrettable situations. If you're disciplined, do your research, and stay vigilant, you save yourself from trouble and regret. Usually, by the time you're at the regret stage, most of the damage is done.

It takes discipline to start and grow a business and more discipline to keep it successful and safeguard it against negligence and complacency. There are many potential pitfalls lurking around, waiting for a chance to invade and destroy your company or your life.

> If you're disciplined, do your research, and stay vigilant, you save yourself from trouble and regret. Usually, by the time you're at the regret stage, most of the damage is done.

You can avoid these pitfalls by finding a competent, reliable, and ethical provider for your background checks and screening services, one that makes it smooth and easy for you to protect your business. A good company isn't afraid to alert you to potential vulnerabilities in your process or policy as they relate to safeguarding your assets. A provider should be experienced, have the necessary credentials, be committed to staying up to date and compliant, and provide you with easy-to-access customer support with timely delivery. This is not one of those items that should be left for "someday." There are seven days in a week, and someday is not one of them!

NO 100 PERCENT SAFEGUARDS
IN BANKING AND MEDICINE

You can try to be careful, but if you open a bank account, the bank has your information. Most people cannot live without a bank account. Despite the many safeguards, accounts can be hacked, and you can end up a victim. Your account or card information will be out there, increasing the risk of a criminal opening an account in your name.

There are not too many people who can say, "I'm foolproof when it comes to this." You can attempt to install all the safeguards, but trusted institutions such as banks or even government agencies may compromise this information.

To make your effort to safeguard your data as comprehensive as possible, you should check your credit, monitor your accounts, and monitor what's out there on the search engines and social media pages.

Different considerations apply when you're examining official entities, such as hospitals and banks. They need to share information, in certain instances, with government agencies for the purpose of monitoring suspects or for complying with the Patriot Act. They may have to file a suspicious activity report.

Sometimes, personal files from a medical office or lab end up in a dumpster, leaving them exposed to theft. Often, employees don't understand how to dispose of such records properly. If they need to hold on to the records, they don't always know how long they should keep them. Once a compliance period is passed, employees need a policy for the proper disposal of medical files and purge of the information they contain. In other words, the documents must be shredded to make sure they don't fall into the wrong hands.

There's a lot you need to do to fight this battle. You must monitor and ask questions to improve your chances of avoiding these perils.

FIGHTING FOR YOUR RIGHT TO PRIVACY

If you really want to fully protect yourself, you have to constantly be vigilant so information that has been gathered is not published, sold, or put online. Some people argue that certain information needs to be out there. We need it to do research, statistics, or verify who have paid their bills or haven't paid their bills.

So what do you do? You have to fight legislation and try to raise a stink. It's an ongoing battle because you don't know what's going to come out next.

We don't want to be paranoid or take it to the extreme, but it's good to be aware of what's going on. The more educated consumers are, the better off they are. When everybody starts to understand the implications of all of this disseminated information, we will understand its long-term consequences better.

Consumers must start identifying those who don't use personal information responsibly and report such cases to the authorities, including the Federal Trade Commission (FTC) and other relevant agencies. Concerned businesses and citizens should talk to their political representatives when they witness actions they feel are illegal. Wherever a legal loophole exists, it's a free-for-all. Europe and Canada have different privacy laws that do not allow the disclosure of as much personal information as US law allows. Obviously, there are instances when disclosure makes sense, but it should only be carried out by entities that have undergone the proper qualification process and whose use of, or purpose for, the information is legally permissible.

Any time you see what you think may be an illegal disclosure of personal data, you can try cleaning up your own data. If you see a breach of confidentiality that affects a lot of people who probably aren't aware of it, you should bring the issue up to the FTC.

Once people know what's at stake, they will be concerned for their own safety and well-being and the safety and well-being of their family, their friends, and society in general.

Once people see the downside of certain actions, they can vote with their wallets and their own behavior.

> Once people know what's at stake, they will be concerned for their own safety and well-being and the safety and well-being of their family, their friends, and society in general.

An interesting trend to watch is the recent increase in start-up companies attempting to build on privacy, search engines that don't keep your Internet history, and even e-mail and messaging services that destroy all online tracks. Social networks are being built that don't keep your pictures. The premise is that because they don't keep such data, no one can ever get it, including the government. Examples of this response to the need for increased privacy include PieceMealSocialNEtwork, DuckDuckGo search engine, and Lavabit e-mail.

While the economic viability, resilience, and demand for these companies are not proven yet, the market itself will dictate the direction which developments will take. When consumers voice their concern, you see products and services come into the market to address that concern. We will see more networks and technology providers addressing privacy, safety, and security issues.

CHAPTER 2

WHO CONTROLS DATA?

"There are only two types of companies: those that
have been hacked, and those that will be."

—Robert S. Mueller III, former FBI director

Data is collected, stored, and disseminated by various entities, including government agencies and federal, state, city, and municipal courts. For example, motor vehicle departments and private entities collect data for health care, drug screening, and other uses. Credit reporting agencies collect payment histories and credit histories. All are responsible for collecting and storing this data properly and disseminating it to those with highly justifiable reasons for obtaining it. Ideally, the collection process should include notifying individuals and obtaining their consent before their personal data is collected and shared. Private entities, hackers, and corporations also collect, aggregate, or otherwise handle many types of data.

For our purposes here, we will focus on data as it relates to background checks and other screening procedures, since our business is in background checks. The principles we will focus on are availability and legitimate access. We will discuss the topics of responsibility, training, consent, and the requirements for disclosure.

COURT RECORDS

Court records originate at the courts where the cases were filed. These can be federal, state, county, city, or municipal courts, depending on the type of case. Generally, they're open to the public, which is why you hear them sometimes referred to as public records. Some of these records, or information contained in them, may be confidential and may have to be kept confidential, depending on such things as jurisdiction.

Examples of what courts shouldn't share with the public include juvenile cases, proceedings related to mental health, SS numbers, and credit information. Sensitive subject matter must not be disclosed without a solid, legal reason for disclosure.

Certain matters, such as paternity proceedings, adoption, protection order files, and the final disposition may be shared, but sometimes, filed details aren't disclosed. Errors can happen at any point.

You'll see this pattern with much of the data that is collected, sold, and shared. It can happen at the point of entry. It can happen during transfer. It can happen during sharing or selling. Courts and government agencies sell this information as well. Database compilers who purchase the data from official agencies resell it to investigators and background check companies that may make mistakes, especially when performing instant searches. For example, they may mistakenly use information that has not been updated. There are consequences for not mitigating these risks and taking appropriate measures to do things correctly, which can include fines, penalties, or lawsuits resulting from violations of FTC or EEOC rules.

DEPARTMENT OF MOTOR VEHICLES

Vehicle registrations and driver/motor vehicle records and histories are kept by the department of motor vehicles (DMV) in each state, and DMV officials and law enforcement have access to them. Sometimes, private entities that aggregate the data and use it to extract other information for vehicle histories or vehicle accident histories, sell that information. A good example of that is Carfax. Anyone who completes a background check on you, whether an employer, a landlord, a lender, or insurance company, will have access to that information.

Of course, there can be errors at many levels. For example, the Indiana Bureau of Motor Vehicles has cost taxpayers over $29 million in refunds because it misclassified vehicles and over-charged or undercharged the owners. The mistakes date back to 2004, but the effects are still being dealt with today.[2]

Sometimes, VIN numbers can be mismatched, which can create hassles when you're trying to get insurance or traveling. For instance, if you're pulled over, further inquiries will ensue, or God forbid, your information may be mismatched with someone who stole a vehicle. It was discovered in Minnesota that some state employees had accessed files for no other purpose than curiosity. They looked up information on a subject of interest, something unrelated to their jobs, such as a girlfriend.

Go to your favorite search engine and look up something such as "DMV records misuse," or "DMV records abuse." You'll pull up stories of what can happen when things go wrong with

---

2 | Tony Cook and Justin L. Mack, "In latest mistake, BMV to issue $29M in refunds," *Indystar*, September 16, 2014, http://www.indystar.com/story/news/politics/2014/09/16/indiana-bmv-issue-m-refunds-motorists/15719711/

the use of data that is normally protected by state and federal laws and procedures that prohibit people without justified access from browsing personal information.

The question becomes one of tracking abuses. You can usually do that through audits. Some of these abuses have been uncovered through access laws. When auditors find individuals who have been looking at records that have nothing to do with their work—for example, male workers who browse women's personal data—they start an investigation.

This happens in the nonbusiness world as well and can result in lawsuits and criminal charges and have a major impact on people's lives.

CREDIT REPORTS

The main credit reporting agencies are Experian, TransUnion, and Equifax, but there are many others. Those with access to them include lenders, insurance companies, landlords, property managers, and anyone who rents something.

When background checks are carried out on job applicants, credit checks must be appropriate and relevant to the job for which the individual is applying. If you're a corporate accountant or a treasurer, you have a legal reason to run a credit check. Sometimes, government agencies may also have a justification for performing certain types of searches or accessing records to assess eligibility for a certain credential or benefit.

The following is an example of the relevance principle:

INFORMATION REQUIREMENTS
FOR SUITABILITY REFERRALS

Issues	Criteria
• Any evidence of dishonesty or fraud in the competitive examination or appointment process (such as falsification of application)	Always refer, regardless of the date of occurrence.
• Any statutory debarment issue • Any loyalty or terrorism issue	Always refer, regardless of the date of occurrence.
Major and substantial issues, including but not limited to • Patterns of conduct (such as a pattern of drug or alcohol abuse, financial irresponsibility, or major liabilities, dishonesty, unemployability due to negligence, misconduct, or criminal conduct) • Other than honorable military discharge • Felony offense • Illegal drug manufacturing, trafficking, or sale • Major honesty issue (such as extortion, armed robbery, embezzlement, perjury) • Serious violent behavior (such as rape, aggravated assault, arson, child abuse, manslaughter) • Sexual misconduct (such as sexual assault, sexual harassment, prostitution) • Illegal use of firearms or explosives • Hatch Act violation • Employment-related conduct involving dishonest, criminal, or violent behavior	Refer all within three years. *For patterns, the conduct may begin prior to, but must extend into, the last three years.*

Issues	Criteria
Moderate issues, including but not limited to • Driving while intoxicated • Drug-related offense (excluding infrequent use or possession of marijuana or marijuana paraphernalia; including arrests or charges for possession of marijuana) • Petty theft or forgery • Assault, criminal mischief, harassment • Employment related misconduct involving insubordination, absenteeism, rules violations	Refer for two or more occurrences within three years. *May be a combination of moderate and minor issues within three years.*
Minor issues, including but not limited to • Minor liquor law violation • Minor traffic violation • Bad check • Minor disruptive conduct (such as disorderly conduct, trespassing, vagrancy, loitering, disturbing the peace) • Minor employment-related misconduct	Refer for three or more occurrences within three years. *May be a combination of these issues within three years.*

For employment purposes, you have to take all of those issues into consideration.

There are spin-off products based on your credit report, including scorecards that landlords use. The credit reporting agencies sell some of these products. They sell the landlords tenant scorecards based on residence histories, lawsuits, and payment histories. Some landlords subscribe to programs in which they report to credit bureaus. In an ideal world, this shouldn't be done without the permission of their tenants, but portions of their reports are sold or shared for various commercial purposes.

Credit reports can contain a lot of your history, including past employers, past addresses, loans you've applied for or you cosigned for, mortgage payment histories, collections-related data, and possibly, even relationships.

Normally, the FTC handles complaints related to credit reporting violations, but sometimes, other consumer agencies can help. If you're curious about this, go to the FTC's website. You can find a lot of useful information about this there and about what should be done in case you were wronged.

Take into account that the stakes are higher when reviewing documents, such as credit reports. Make sure you're not being unfair, because in a bad economy, a lot of people have to deal with credit issues, difficulty in finding work, and the challenges of continuing to pay their clients. Employers can help break the vicious cycle that affects those with bad credit. If they make decisions based on recent bad credit alone, they just contribute to this vicious cycle.

One of the biggest issues surrounding credit reports is the risk of identity theft. You should always monitor your credit. At minimum, review your yearly free reports with all three of the major credit reporting agencies. It's becoming cheaper to do this monitoring, which alerts you to applications made under your name and inquiries you didn't initiate, giving you a little bit more time to react.

Otherwise, you'll have to rely on other signs that your identity has been stolen, such as getting unexpected calls from collectors asking you for money you didn't spend. Your credit card may be declined. Your insurance company may reject your claim, alleging you've used all your coverage when, in fact, you haven't used any.

Monitor your accounts as frequently as possible to check for transactions you don't recognize. They may indicate use of your information by someone unauthorized to do so. That person may only have your card, which you can usually cancel with a phone call. Most of the time, you can obtain a refund, depending on your bank's policies and the type of card involved, debit or credit. If you get to this point, the damage has been done, and you have a steep hill to climb from here.

Monitor your accounts as frequently as possible to check for transactions you don't recognize. They may indicate use of your information by someone unauthorized to do so.

If you get to the point where the IRS informs you that duplicate tax returns have been filed with your information or your bank representative says, "Hey, there's crazy stuff going on with your account. Is this really you?" you've waited too long. Some banks are very proactive if an activity is different from their customers' normal pattern. They usually have a fraud department that will notify customers of unusual activity. They may freeze a card until they've talked to the customer and verified the transaction was made by that customer and no one else.

For instance, if bank customers don't travel much, the transactions they make in one geographical area will become a pattern that is noted by bank staff. When those customers travel abroad without notifying their bank, bank staff may ask them to verify their travel. Proactive banks may stop all transactions while they check a customer's identity.

SOCIAL SECURITY

The Social Security Administration allows you, your employers, and credit bureaus access to your SS records. The administration shares this information with credit-card-related services, financial services, medical offices, hospitals, schools, and colleges.

Many other agencies can have access because SS numbers are unique identifiers for tracking and assessing benefits eligibility, bestowing a privilege or license, and for other official purposes. Most of the time, the number serves only for identification, but errors, mismatches, and unauthorized access can happen.

Errors have occurred when states and even the Social Security Administration have misclassified information, including adding living people to the Social Security Death Index, which tracks deceased people and notes their death in their SS account. Thousands, if not millions, of people have been erroneously classified as dead, and the consequences are immense because those people's services and benefits are cut off. Their information is published in the Social Security Administration's Death Master File, which exposes their SS information, putting it outside the protections received by the living.

Some people had to fight an uphill battle to fix that error. Usually, it's easy to fix by simply going in person to a local SS office and showing the staff various types of identity documents.

In some instances, victims of this error may have to track down whoever reported their death to the Social Security Administration to obtain the erroneous death certificate and a signed statement. Then, they have to take the statement to the Social Security Administration. After that, they must contact the credit reporting agencies and wherever the news of their "death" may have been disseminated. They have to go after the false information and correct it. During that period, besides suffering all of the headache and added risk of identity theft, these people could lose their government benefits. Their credit could also be affected, resulting in closed bank accounts and bounced checks.

EDUCATION RECORDS

Education records are kept by schools, from elementary and secondary schools to colleges, trade schools, and many other educational institutions. They can share information because, as students move through the different stages of education, they need to prove where they've previously studied and that they've completed prerequisites for the next level of their education. You should be aware of this and know that educational verification will take place if you give consent. Background check companies, acting on behalf of employers, should be able to get access to that information, with your consent. In some instances, law enforcement can do so as well.

In some areas, the state secretary of education manages educational records. Sometimes, the controller general or the FCC will have that job, and sometimes, it's done on a case-by-case basis.

It's not, normally, a good practice to put a student's SS number on IDs. Another number should be used. Most universities have now replaced SS numbers on IDs with another unique, or primary, identification number that they have issued. Details are covered in the Federal Education Records and Privacy Act or the Buckley Amendment. These actions should be carried out with the consent of the student, with minimum standards for the protection of all of this information.

Some states and local governments add other protections or laws, and some of the details of protection are covered by the Federal Privacy Act of 1974. But protection can also be affected by state laws and also by the Freedom of Information Act.

Regarding education and degrees, it's always good to verify that applicants actually earned the degrees and licenses listed on their resumes. Employers and human resources professionals have to be consistent and responsible with all of this information, and a lot of the rules we previously mentioned apply here too. The higher the level of education achieved, the more you want to verify. There have been cases of Fortune 500 companies' executives claiming they had degrees when they didn't.

In 2006 it was discovered that Radio Shack's CEO had lied. He said he had two college degrees, but he only had one. He ended up resigning. Bausch and Lomb's former CEO claimed he had an MBA from New York University, but later, it came out that he only started but never finished that program. He didn't lose his job at that time but gave up his bonus of $1 million. He is no longer with that company.

WHERE ARE THE REGULATIONS, AND WHO IS WATCHING THE WATCHER?

There are people and activists who continually wonder whether we do enough about privacy—namely, who is watching the watcher? Should we have a regulator for each industry or an overall government entity that oversees management of information? For each one source of information, there is at least one entity that tries to oversee its use and distribution. How well they're doing their job, however, is a big question.

In the United States it's a combination of self-regulation, self-policing, and the market that drive information distribution. There are risks involved if you are found to be mismanaging information, and the media are aggressive. Activists who uncover some of these things and, maybe, the precedents they set will scare everybody into doing the right thing.

Some privacy laws already exist, such as the Privacy Act, the Family Educational Rights and Privacy Act (FERPA), FCRA, and the Civil Rights Act, while the EEOC, and the US Department of Labor are also resources.

You may obtain a DMV record containing information such as a SS number, or your SS trace may include additional information that overlaps with the DMV data.

There should be disclosure. Employers, landlords, and even websites should inform you, whenever you're being asked for personal or sensitive information, about disclosure, whether the information they are requesting is mandatory, why they need it, and whether they have the authority to ask for it.

OTHER TYPES OF SCREENING
AND DUE DILIGENCE

Worker's Compensation

Workers' compensation records are usually kept by the state or in the state where the claim was filed. Workers' compensation is considered public information, though some states may have stronger rules than others on what gets published. This information can be used by insurance companies and for employment purposes, but it must be used very carefully, if at all. Normally, it should not be used unless in conjunction with something like the Americans with Disabilities Act (ADA), and some state laws are there to protect the applicant from discrimination. Employees who have filed a legally valid claim for worker's compensation shouldn't have that claim used against them, because such a claim is within their rights. But there can be abuses with just about any situation. Workers' compensation records should only be used to clear up concerns about whether a claim was ultimately ruled to be valid.

Employers trying to evaluate disabled candidates' ability to do the job should give candidates the opportunity to show they can do the job with reasonable accommodations. The American with Disabilities Act explains what employers are allowed and not allowed to do. It also covers the rights of disabled applicants and employees.

An employer's policies, processes, and procedures have to be consistent regarding worker's compensation or hiring an employee convicted of a misdemeanor. For instance, if you do not hire an applicant, because that person was convicted of a misdemeanor, you cannot now hire somebody who has been convicted of a misdemeanor but is of a different race, age, or sex from the applicant you did not hire. Following the law and being fair and ethical is what should govern your actions. Usually, people will see whether you've taken reasonable care and have done the right thing or skirted the proper procedure. There needs to be consistency in everything from recruitment and on-boarding to development and advancement opportunities, employment or continued employment conditions, managers and owner training, termination policies, and the right of candidates to dispute inaccuracies in their reports.

Bankruptcy Records

Bankruptcy records are kept with the courts, normally, in the jurisdiction where they're filed, which can be where the claimant resides or wherever the claimant chooses to file them. This information can be packaged and sold, and then it's public record. The federal courts uniformly report to a system called Pacer, which is viewable to the public.

Who gets access? You can get access to it. It's a major resource for credit reporting companies and financial lenders, including mortgage lenders. Anyone who wants to look up public records can find this information. As with most court records, errors can happen, but they are mostly confined to filing time limits and disclosures.

For instance, documents may be out of date or misfiled, or they've been filed in bankruptcy cases to avoid legitimate responsibilities, hide assets, or transfer ownership. Such cases can sometimes turn into a criminal matter involving federal prosecutors.

Drug Screenings

Drug screenings can take place at many different places, from drug screening collection agencies, health centers, and hospitals to the doctor's office. Consumers can buy home test kits and send a sample—for example, a urine or hair sample—to a lab. Some tests are instant. For more official purposes, a qualified drug-screening agency should be used. Such agencies usually have the right equipment and are compliant with health and safety codes. They have trained personnel and may also have a medical review officer who can analyze the test results based on the purpose of the test. There has to be a legitimate need for this, and it has to be relevant. Again, errors can be made. You should let the medical review officer know of any medications that may skew the result. Regulators include the US Department of Health and Human Services (DHHS), state departments of health, and other local agencies.

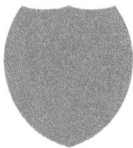

> Employers should make sure they are familiar with FCRA rules, the Health Insurance Portability and Accountability Act (HIPAA), and EEOC and ADA rules in addition to relevant federal and local laws.

Drug testing is commonplace. The affects of drug use on workers' productivity, absenteeism, turnover rate, and on the operation of dangerous machinery have long been a concern. These factors can result in increased workers' compensation costs and claims. Employers who perform regular drug screens can say they provide safe and healthy environments for the employees.

Some of them do postaccident testing for drugs in the employee's system at the time of an accident.

Issues that can arise from screenings include discrimination issues, employee protection issues, civil rights issues, or violations of the American Disability Act.

Legalization of marijuana is an issue that's still in flux, and it's a hotly debated topic. Employees with a medical need worry about the stigma, discrimination, and additional scrutiny. Reports indicate employers in states such as Colorado are ramping up drug testing policies in response to the legalization. Employers, on the other hand, worry about how this will influence productivity and liability at their business.

Employers should make sure they are familiar with FCRA rules, the Health Insurance Portability and Accountability Act (HIPAA), and EEOC and ADA rules in addition to relevant federal and local laws. Employers have a responsibility not to discriminate and to be aware of all the civil laws and antidiscrimination laws and disability laws. They cannot even make subjective, irrelevant notes while interviewing candidates; their notes have to be relevant to the job.

International Searches

In a lot of the other countries, private data is gathered and maintained more often by government than private entities. Government and culture have a significant impact on regulation. In some countries, the public has no control over the use of personal data. In other countries, technology is so far behind that public use of personal data hasn't become much of an issue. In European and other developed countries, privacy laws are well established.

Gathering Information from Other Countries

International searches can be complicated. Some countries are still dependent upon paper filing systems, and there are issues of legality and cultural appropriateness. Some foreign governments can impose unfamiliar restrictions on things, such as cross-border transfers or the type of information that is allowed to be gathered and reported about their citizens.

Depending on the country you are contacting, it may take weeks or months to receive requested information. Most countries have data that is classified at the municipal or provincial level. To access this information, you may be required to contact local investigative personnel or resources such as prosecutors' offices and police departments.

Identifiers (IDs) are different in different parts of the world. In some countries, people write their first name first, followed by their family name. Birthdays and other important dates can also be written in different ways. Be aware of whether the first number you see is the month of birth or the day of birth.

In some areas, you can only access a name and address because other information is not available, not recorded in case details, or not disclosed to the researcher or investigator. You may need to be familiar with a subject's country-specific national ID number, since SS numbers do not exist everywhere. Countries outside the USA have their own versions of SS numbers, including identification such as student IDs and workers' numbers.

There are places where you can only refer to police records after certain required procedures are completed. Completing those prerequisites to access police records occasionally requires some work. Sometimes, only the subject of the investigation can request these documents.

Depending on where you are located on the globe, you might be able to find background check products equivalent to those available in the United States. International supplement product searches include the Terrorist Watch List. There are specially designated national and financial crime lists, as well as politically exposed people (PEP) lists. Politically exposed people are individuals who hold positions of importance in their respective countries.

Due to problems with stolen passports, databases have been created to store this information. Serious crimes committed in other countries will also show up at foreign news or press services. A Google search and a translation tool will help you search news stories.

Employers are required to verify that a job applicant has the legal right to work in the United States. Products exist to locate and verify such information.

Complications occur when you're not only translating into a different language but using a different alphabet. Chinese, Japanese, Hindi, and Arabic use characters that people in the Western world might not be familiar with.

When you are working with information in a different language, or from abroad in general, it is important to be familiar with those countries' processes and with the language itself. It helps to know the details of local IDs and identification systems.

Be aware of how to write the name of the person you are researching. Some names, depending on the language, can be spelled different ways but still apply to one individual. Mistakes can happen when attempting to translate names phonetically, especially when using unfamiliar alphabets. You don't want to research the wrong person because you tried to sound out the spelling of the name in English and spelled it incorrectly.

A practical example is the name Stephen. Some people spell it Steven. Some people spell it Stephen. Stephen Jones and Steven Jones, however, are two very different individuals.

Mistakes waste time and cause delays in the delivery of the correct information. Turnaround times can be lengthy in certain countries. Before you submit any requests, make sure you have everything that is required by the country you're dealing with and you submit all necessary materials at the same time. When information needs to be repeatedly passed back and forth between countries, it may add an unreasonable amount of time to the process. If you know what you need to send before you send it, you will save yourself a lot of time.

Most countries have one or two laws that cover the entire privacy issue in all its aspects, whereas the United States has multiple state and federal laws and regulations and, as mentioned earlier, gray areas that no jurisdiction covers, as well as overlap.

It is easier to get personal information in the United States than it is in a lot of the other countries. Is this a good thing? Opinions vary.

It is easier to get personal information in the United States than it is in a lot of the other countries. Is this a good thing?

Opinions vary. Some people completely distrust the government and do not approve of any information gathering. Others are practical and understand how these things work. Some people are totally indifferent and consider it a matter of no importance.

DIFFERING OPINIONS ON PRIVACY PROTECTION

If you were to survey people about their feelings on information gathering, you would see a pattern of influences on their opinions. Backgrounds, political tendencies, belief in the Bill of Rights, and similar factors can determine which end of this spectrum they occupy.

Then there are market forces. You would think most corporations would be against greater privacy. In some instances, increased privacy safeguards their intellectual property and their copyrights, trademarks, and trade secrets.

When you tell most people they will benefit from sharing information or they will help to limit fraud by sharing information, which, in turn, lessens the cost of products and services—insurance rates, for example—then background and credit checks make sense to them.

One has to always be alert to, and vigilant with, privacy issues, background checks, information gathering, dissemination, and sharing and selling, which have become moneymakers for a lot of people. It's become very cheap to collect personal data, store it, segregate it, aggregate it, and use it for intelligence gathering, market research, consumer behavior, consumer tracking, and much more.

Privacy involves many overlapping issues, whether background checks, your online habits, or safeguarding your computer at home. You have to be alert. You have to be vigilant. You have to be educated as much as possible about what you need to do to safeguard your privacy.

Privacy can be exploited for illegal purposes, which can increase the cost of access to information that could otherwise be useful, whether to create better products or start new businesses.

"Who did the background check on him?"

CHAPTER 3

Pitfalls: Are You Off the Rails?

nder the FCRA and state laws, you may be notified after your credit report has been publicly shared or before it's shared. You can request a copy. Most of the rules now require that you be provided with a copy or at least the option to request a copy. Typically, your consent must be secured and a copy provided to you if negative or adverse information is going to be used in decision making. You have the right to know where the negative information was obtained, which then allows you to get a copy of the report and review it for accuracy and to compare notes. You receive what's called an adverse action notice, and you have the ability to dispute the information.

The FCRA determines what should and should not be used and what should and should not be reported. Does that mean the wrong information still gets disseminated and reported? Yes, it does. There are no guarantees that an employer or decision maker will admit a lack of qualifications or experience led to the wrong decision.

When it comes to companies that lie about the reason for their decision, it's a question of who gets caught and who doesn't. Different people respond to different deterrents. Were they concerned with doing the right thing? That's the main reason people make appropriate choices. Others don't want to risk losing their reputations because, recently, action lawsuits have been popping up everywhere.

There are obvious cases in which a court determined a judgment against a company accused of violating the rules. These companies used the wrong information, did not use the information they should have used, did not let the applicant know they had a report, did not identify the report, or did not give the applicant the opportunity to look at the report.

A recent settlement related to FCRA involved Publix supermarkets in a case filed in a Tennessee federal court. An article published in Tampa Bay Business Journal covered the story in which Publix agreed to settle the class-action lawsuit for $6.8 million, while simultaneously denying wrongdoing.[3]

Securing consent is a good example. Big companies have gotten into hot water, been sued, and then lost cases because they included disclosure and consent information in the applicant's job application. They buried it among other information so it could be easily missed. This is a good example of the constant updates that are made to the FCRA. Information about disclosure and consent should be detailed in a separate, clear document that states exactly

---

3 | Solomon, Salem, "Publix pays $6.8M to settle suit," *The Tampa Bay Business Journal*, October 29, 2014, http://www.bizjournals.com/tampabay/blog/morning-edition/2014/10/publix-pays-6-8m-to-settle-suit.html

who, what, and where: what information is being gathered, what it's going to be used for, and where it's being gathered from. That way, applicants know exactly what's going to happen. They're not blindly signing a document in which they may have missed that statement that reads, "We're going to get this particular report about you and this and this and this."

Big companies have gotten into hot water, been sued, and then lost cases because they included disclosure and consent information in the applicant's job application.

In a few states, such as California, Oklahoma, and Minnesota, an applicant can elect to receive a copy of the report when it is supplied to the employer. In other states, a report is only accessed when adverse action is to be taken.

If you are a California employer, and regardless of whether you conduct the background check yourself or hire an outside company, you must also:

- Give the individual who is being checked notice of the right to ask for a copy of any background report;

- Give notice of the right to know the nature and scope of a background check;

- Give contact information for the screening company.

Employer's Obligations	FCRA	California ICRA Act
Employee's permission	Must be obtained on a separate document before a report is requested. Permission is not necessary for subsequent reports. Special permission is required for medical information.	Must be obtained on a separate document at any time a report is requested. Special permission is required for medical information.
If employee is suspected of wrongdoing	Same procedures for consent required.	Consent is not required.
Notice of rights, for example to dispute information, to review files	Must be given before an adverse action is taken against the applicant or current employee.	Must be given at the time a background check is requested and permission is obtained from the employee.
Copy of report	Must be offered at the time of a notice of intended adverse action.	Must be offered at the time permission is obtained to get the background check report.
Penalties	Actual damages up to $1,000. Punitive damages, costs, and attorney fees (willful). Actual damages, costs, and attorney fees for negligent noncompliance.	Actual damages, but no less than $10,000. Punitive damages for grossly negligent or willful conduct; attorney fees, and costs. Note: 2003 legislation, AB 1399, signed by the governor on July 31, 2003, reduced penalties.

As illustrated by this chart from Privacy Rights Clearing-house—a California nonprofit corporation who lists their mission as: "to engage, educate and empower individuals to protect their privacy. We identify trends and communicate our findings to advocates, policymakers, industry, media and consumers."[4]

PROPER USE OF DATA

Mistakes can happen even at the court level.

We have had situations in which the clerk of the court provided the wrong or mismatched information, but because proper notice and disclosure procedure was followed, the applicant was able to bring it up with the court, correct the information, and rectify the situation.

Brokers of information and people who aggregate the information, gather it, sell it, and resell it can also make mistakes. It's not reasonable to search every county in the United States, so when doing a background search on a job applicant, just search those counties where they have lived and the aliases they've used and then supplement this information with other things, depending on the requirements of the position.

An employer or researcher can do a nationwide database search. Let's say a case you are researching comes up in New Hampshire. You have to go to the court identified in the database to see if the case was actually processed there. If the information

4 | "Small Business Owner Background Check Guide," Privacy Rights Clearing-house, August 2003, revised December 2014, https://www.privacyrights.org/small-business-owner-background-check-guide

is out of date or there was a mismatch, the case record could, somehow, have ended up there, even though, in fact, the court didn't handle the case. Sometimes, when the database information is not up to date, and by the time you look at the case record, the case has been dismissed and can't be used.

There may have been a violation of probation, which could dramatically change the disposition of the case, which, in turn, would determine your response.

You're supposed to seek consent from your applicants before you do a background check and before certain types of searches. You're also supposed to give them adverse action notice if you use your gathered information against them. Ideally, they should have a chance to review it and dispute the claims if they are not correct.

> We all have a responsibility to give these matters their due attention and to be thoughtful and responsible when we examine these cases.

This usually applies to most types of searches, including motor vehicle records, credit reports, sex offender, and other database searches. You have to thoroughly vet the information and double-check it. You must look at the relevance, the seriousness, and the gravity of the case. You have to really use information responsibly.

The court system doesn't always get it right. It's difficult to overturn a lot of court decisions, even when common sense says the outcome should be otherwise. Everyone agrees people have to negotiate a lot of bureaucracy and jump through hoops to clear their name.

Sometimes, they successfully clear their name, and sometimes they never get their life back. We all have a responsibility to give these matters their due attention and to be thoughtful and responsible when we examine these cases.

HANDLING YOUR OWN
INFORMATION PROPERLY

Your lifetime's worth of data, electronic records, paper documents, and all kinds of other records can have huge consequences for you, as a consumer, if not handled correctly. On the other hand, what if you wake up one day and find all of your data wiped out? Bank information gone, driver's license information gone, bank or health history information gone—all the data you take for granted has gone. How would you function?

We have all these records we maintain ourselves at our homes, records that travel through the mail, and records on file with third parties. You have a file with your dentist. You have a file with your doctor. You have a file with your local insurance agent. You have files for health benefits. You have files with brokers. Realtors may have files that you filled out some time ago, and they didn't dispose of the information.

Sometimes, we mishandle information ourselves. Sometimes, if we don't dispose of documents properly ourselves, we give the dumpster divers the information. Dumpster divers know whether the offices they service handle a lot of SS numbers and date of birth information. Some jurisdictions have moved to limit the extent to which personal information is collected in different records. In the past, it was common practice for SS numbers to be listed in court records and property ownership documents. A lot of agencies and jurisdictions have started blocking out that data to safeguard it. With that being said, you can still find SS information in a lot records.

If it's physical information you're keeping, on forms or in files, safeguard it, even in your own home. Make sure you have certain areas that have more controlled access. If you don't need a document, shred or burn it to the point where it cannot be read. Don't just tear it into pieces and throw it in the garbage. Someone can easily take it out, piece it back together, and use the information.

Ask companies about their policies. What are their record retention policies? What is their record disposal policy? You shouldn't give out personal information to anyone you're not really sure about and whose credibility you haven't determined. Sometimes, small companies go out of business and leave everything behind, which risks personal data falling into the wrong hands. Nowadays, if the wrong people get hold of a paper document containing personal data, eventually, they'll get into the electronic world to try to use it.

You have to watch for all those signs of identity theft that we've talked about. You'll see that fewer people are publishing their phone numbers. Some will even pay to remove a published number if necessary.

Mishandling can happen to anybody. Mistakes can happen at any level. You can make mistakes. An employer can make mistakes. A court can make mistakes. A government agency can make mistakes. You have to be informed, and you have to be educated about all of these different things. There is not one person who is the one and only expert in all of this, because the world is continually changing.

If you maintain your safeguards and do reasonable, occasional monitoring, you should be safer than most. It just becomes a case of the odds. Monitoring stacks the odds against your identity being stolen or your sensitive and personal information falling into the wrong hands.

PROTECTING YOUR DIGITAL INFORMATION

Safeguarding data means keeping it under lock and key. We're talking about both electronic and nonelectronic documents. Don't keep your login information right next to the computer. Don't save your login information on the computer. Lock that computer. Make it password protected.

You have to make sure you have antivirus, up-to-date software, firewalls, and strong passwords. Do not give your first name as your password or your son's name or your house number. Make your passwords difficult to crack. Get a little bit creative with your passwords to make them stronger. Come up with your own language. The further away you are from the obvious answers, the safer you are. Systems, codes, and hackers can set programs to crack passwords by running all kinds of combinations of different words. Hopefully, you'll never be on the receiving end of that activity, because it's sophisticated stuff that brings down big companies.

If you really need the data, store it in the right places, secure it, make sure it's password protected and you have controlled access. Don't open anything you don't recognize, whether it's a link or an attachment. Dishonest people are getting very smart with hacking. The earlier spammers just sold products and made money. Now that spamming has become illegal, or at least taboo, most spamming is done with criminal intentions. People have sobered up to a lot of the scams, such as the Nigerian scam, or claims that they won a lottery in Spain or in London. Since most of the general public now knows about such scams, smart criminals have begun to spoof institutional entities, even the IRS website. (Spoofing is an impersonation of a friend or contact by a malicious entity using that person's e-mail address to send you a malicious link or attachment.) They're spoofing your bank's website from where they may send you an e-mail, and they may even have a website that looks exactly like your bank's site. The IRS scam, for example, claims to need your information to fix an error or to send you your refund. The IRS will never send you a request by e-mail to verify your information, nor will a bank, normally. If you didn't initiate that phone call or that e-mail, be suspicious. In any event, never share important information in an e-mail message.

If you use your private computer on a public network, be aware of what information you share in public. When you're not in a perfect situation, avoid going into your accounts. Some browsers have a default setting to save login information and numbers. You have to make sure you don't check, or uncheck, a "Keep me logged in" or "Save my login information" box.

Make sure you purge regularly, both physical and electronic information. Check your browser settings to make sure that your computer is not storing everything you're doing, and adjust your settings to the right privacy settings. Every now and then, it's a good practice to delete all your temporary Internet files, the history, the downloads, and browser information. If you're in a public place, working on your own computer on a secure network, and you've taken all those precautions, watch out for people who might be looking over your shoulders.

> **With the widespread use of wireless spots and smartphones, you can expect to see more and more people trying to intercept data and steal it.**

Unfortunately, people who are trained criminals are very quick at this and know exactly how to take a snapshot of what they need. Before you realize it, they have your name and your SS number. If you make it a habit to take precautions, it betters your chances of keeping your data safe.

With the widespread use of wireless spots and smartphones, you can expect to see more and more people trying to intercept data and steal it. With that will come more people trying to develop ways to protect against the theft of information.

These issues have an interesting history. The first patent for a voice scrambler was issued probably within the same year, or a year after, the phone was invented. There is always something being developed; the chase is always on. Who's ahead at any given time?

Just keep an eye out and be informed. Take these safety precautions, both physically and also on computers and electronic devices. If you do these things, you shouldn't be paranoid, but if you don't, you should be paranoid.

PRECAUTION IN A NUTSHELL

You need to be worried about other people getting documents showing your unique and sensitive identifiers, as well as anything you don't want anybody to see. Any correspondence from your doctor or your hospital is also private and sensitive.

I'm worried about papers that have a combination of a few identifiers. I'm not worried about my name and address. If something comes in the mail that identifies my name and address and nothing else, that's just information that anyone can find by searching me on the Internet or by picking up a phone book. I put that sort of information in the recycle bin.

If a credit card company sends you an offer on a form you can fill out, that's something to be concerned about. There are credit card scammers who try to get you to transfer all your credit card balances.

Anything that somebody can use to harm you, that's not already out there, that's not known, not obvious or public, is what should be the determining factor regarding what you protect.

Your name and address are easy for people to find out, but things get complicated when those details are combined with your complete date of birth and your SS number written on a document somewhere. I don't carry my SS number in my wallet. If you lose your wallet, you must call all your credit card providers and cancel the cards. You can't cancel your SS number and just get a new one. If people get that information, either physically or electronically, they have everything they need to take advantage of you.

Don't write your SS number or carry your SS card in your wallet, and don't put them in places that are accessible to others. Some people already have your date of birth, so just make sure they don't get another piece of personal information. Anything containing those two pieces of information is ready for use—for example, checks with your bank account information or credit cards. They are a one-stop shop for an identity thief.

CHAPTER 4

HIPAA:
THE DANGERS

T he Health Insurance Portability and Accountability Act (HIPAA) is supposed to establish a national standard for security rules regarding physical and electronic information. It's supposed to establish the safeguards for the security, confidentiality, and integrity of the information. These sensitive records are for official, relevant use only and not for casual browsing by health-care facility employees.

In a class-action suit, in July 2013, the Superior Court of Marion County, Indiana, ordered Walgreens to pay $1.44 million. Walgreens appealed, but the Court of Appeals of Indiana upheld the decision on November 2014. A Walgreens pharmacist looked up the records of her husband's ex-girlfriend because she suspected his ex-girlfriend had infected him with a sexually transmitted disease. She found the information, and her husband confronted the ex, who, of course, was livid and notified Walgreens. "This should not be happening," she said. "People like this should not be having access to my information." Some days after the ex-girlfriend notified the pharmacy, the pharmacist accessed the information again, so the ex sued for Walgreens' failure to protect the information and train and supervise its personnel regarding the limits to access. The jury awarded the plaintiff 80 percent of those damages. Whenever a lawsuit is involved, regardless of the outcome, the company sustains monetary or reputational damages at minimum.

The HIPAA came into effect in April 2003 and only applies to complaints filed after that date.

One has to be familiar with all of the specifics and also the entities covered by HIPAA. The covered entities are health-care providers, anybody who administers health plans, and any clearinghouse, doctors, psychologists, dentists, clinics, nursing homes, pharmacies, HMOs, and government programs that manage, pay, or work in health care.

HIPAA rules and the regulations must be followed not only by the agencies that are directly governed by them but also by any of their vendors, or their business partners, or third parties they work with.

These entities focus on the intake of information. The input has to be done responsibly, and maintained, and safeguarded responsibly. Disseminating or sharing it with people they are required to share it with has to be done responsibly. The rules and the regulations must be followed not only by the agencies that are directly governed by them but also by any of their vendors, or their business partners, or third parties they work with.

They have to establish commitment from these entities as well as compliance. The Office for Civil Rights (OCR) educates and trains people in compliance and is also responsible for investigating possible breaches. It takes complaints and may refer to the US Department of Justice if criminal activity is found. It may fine for violations and apply the breach notification requirements to notify affected entities of a security breach. These entities can include individuals, the secretary of the DHHS or, if relevant, the FTC, and in some instances, the media.

Everybody seems to be getting into trouble with the notifications. When businesses, landlords, or other entities do background checks or credit checks or research a particular person, many of them don't understand they're responsible for notifying the consumer of what's going on with this information. They must inform the consumer of everything including why the data is being collected, what is being done with it, with whom it will be shared, and when a decision based on it will be made. They are also supposed to get permission to share it with another entity.

If you would like to review a more comprehensive list of the HIPAA-covered entities, you can go to the DHHS (www.dhhs.org) and look at the Code of Federal Regulations (CFR), parts 160 and 103. The rules of the DHHS also concern nondiscrimination in addition to those of the OCR.

The Patient Safety and Quality Improvement Act (PSQIA) of 2005 contributes to patient safety laws. The PDQIA also speaks to voluntary reporting systems such as information that may be required to improve quality or speed of care for individuals or for general research or study purposes. Information may be required or optional. Patients and other affected entities need to know the difference between what's required (mandatory) in order to receive a service and what's optional (given voluntarily). You often need authorizations and disclosure notices and maintenance and protection of the information you use and later dispose of when you're not required to keep it anymore.

Patients and other affected entities need to know the difference between what's required (mandatory) in order to receive a service and what's optional (given voluntarily).

There are federal laws, state laws, and industry requirements or specialty requirements for a specific industry. You'll see that some of these laws and rules often intersect and supplement each other. Gray areas necessitate making the right judgment.

Another entity that intersects with PSQIA in some of its aspects is FERPA. You can find out more information about this at: ww2.ed.gov/ferpa.

These laws and regulations help set boundaries for when two distinct groups, dealing with different types of documents, work together. They help to define which of those records will be more suitable for public access—for example, education records—and which are more closely controlled, such as medical records. An example of such a situation would be that of a health-care facility working with a university clinic. A hospital that runs a clinic on behalf of the university may have some documents that fall into the education records category. Patient safety organizations (PSOs) also contribute, as well as the DHHS, which you may hear referred to as HHS.

The OCR, as we mentioned, brings criminal cases to the attention of the US Department of Justice. The situations might range from negligence to willful criminal activity. When the Department of Justice finds violations, it seeks voluntary compliance involving recognition of the problem and action to address it with a plan and the establishment of rules, training, and software updates.

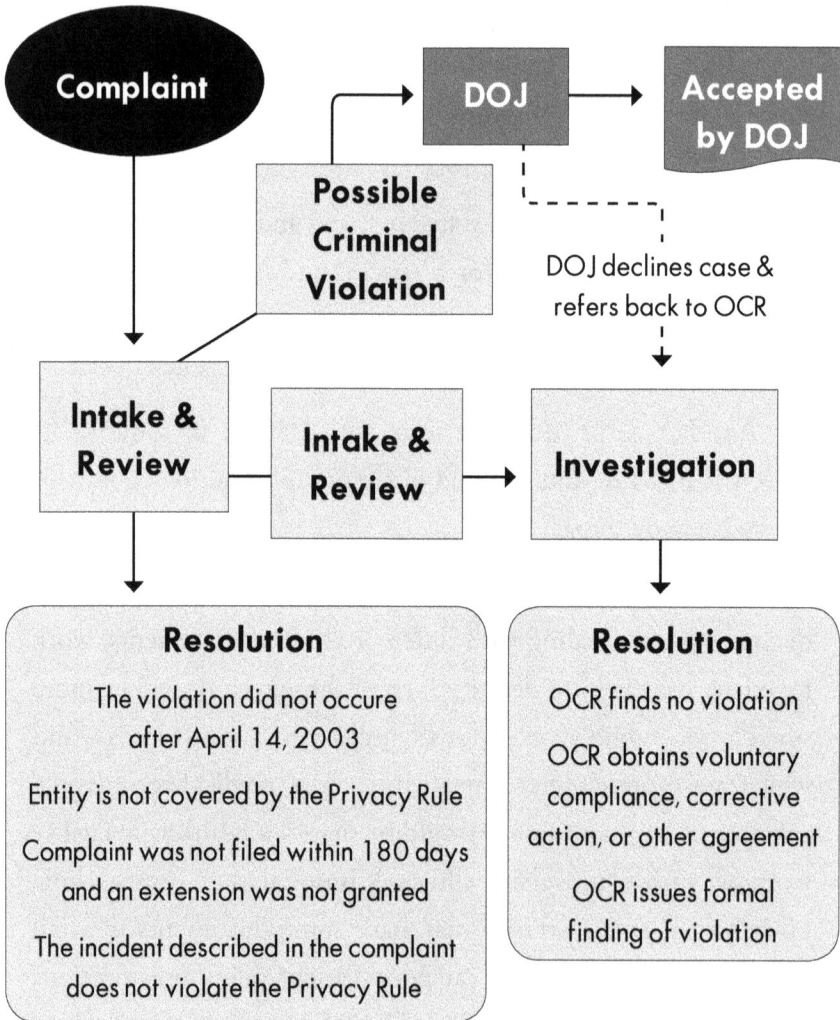

Complaint

DOJ → **Accepted by DOJ**

Possible Criminal Violation

DOJ declines case & refers back to OCR

Intake & Review

Intake & Review → **Investigation**

Resolution

The violation did not occure after April 14, 2003

Entity is not covered by the Privacy Rule

Complaint was not filed within 180 days and an extension was not granted

The incident described in the complaint does not violate the Privacy Rule

Resolution

OCR finds no violation

OCR obtains voluntary compliance, corrective action, or other agreement

OCR issues formal finding of violation

Image Source: http://www.hhs.gov/ocr/privacy/hipaa/enforcement/process/

Since April 2003, the OCR has received a ton of complaints, and 96 percent of them were resolved. After investigation, OCR may deem the charge inapplicable or establish that no rules were actually violated, or the OCR may resolve the issue through enforcement, which subjects the violator to intense scrutiny and determines where changes must be made.

Many complaints concern a violation. The OCR secures compliance once the cause of the violation has been addressed, which usually means processes and/or procedures must be corrected. In 10,390 cases, the OCR found no violations were incurred. There were 63,424 cases that were not eligible for enforcement.[5] The reasons included such minor infractions as missing a deadline, which can happen, for example, when a complainant has 180 days to file a complaint but fails to do within that time frame.

DISCLOSURES, COMPLIANCE, AND LACK THEREOF

Many violations seem to center on disclosure or lack of disclosure. Medical staff fails to disclose the right information to the patient or disclosed it to the wrong patient without the right permissions or didn't safeguard the patient's personal information or didn't provide the patient access when they should have provided it or didn't protect the patient's information correctly or failed to inform the patient of available options and alternatives. This goes back to an earlier discussion of what's required, what's optional,

5 | "Enforcement Highlights," US Department of Health & Human Services, August 31, 2014, http://www.hhs.gov/ocr/privacy/hipaa/enforcement/highlights/08312014.html

what happens if information isn't received, and what happens when information is provided.

You have to be familiar with the limitations of compliance with state and federal laws, such as pre-existing conditions and other possible exclusions, time limits for the use of information, coverage requirements, the provision of certificates and special enrollment rights, discrimination, and prohibitions.

Companies have gotten into trouble for leaving details on answering machines, because anybody can hear that message. You have to make sure the message gets to the right person. Otherwise, there is the risk that someone else will access and publicly share the information. Whether to share their information is up to the patients, but you definitely don't want to be the one to share it on their behalf. Even when patients give specific instructions to doctors' offices to not leave messages, those instructions can get lost in the shuffle. A good practice here is to make sure you address this issue with the patients and don't disregard their preferences. I have seen forms that specifically ask this question so medical staff know if they can leave a message or not.

There was one incident in which an HMO shared a member's personal health information with a disability insurance company without the consent or authorization of the patient. They didn't secure the right form. They used a form intended for a different purpose. Although it contained a small section on health information, the language was not sufficiently clear.

Forms have to be clear about what will be shared when and with whom. Failure to provide notice of privacy practices is not unusual. You have to be transparent, and you have to inform people that you are collecting information on them. As mentioned before, the more sensitive the information is, the more care must be exercised when dealing with it.

HIPAA rules and state statutes address the need for health-care entities to share certain information with patients and not charge patients unreasonable fees to get access to copies of their own records. There are rules stating costs should only include copy, preparation, and postage fees. They cannot be arbitrary. Information seekers cannot become profit centers that charge people for their own personal information.

There was an instance in which a hospital released a patient's skull X-ray (considered protected health information) after an accident. The hospital staff treated the patient and then shared this information with the media under the guise that it was a unique condition the public should be informed about. They failed to do it properly and make sure the patient was okay with it. The main issue in this case was that the information could be easily attributed to this particular patient because the accident had been in the news.

If the hospital had wanted to share the information for research purposes or some other common good, the patient might have agreed to it.

Problems like these can come up in writing, in electronic format, or just from verbal conversation. It's not a good practice to discuss personal information in public, and the same precaution applies here. If you're sitting in the doctor's waiting room, the medical personnel are not supposed to come out and discuss your personal information in front of the other patients in the room. They must take you into a private office that's secure.

Believe it or not, complaints have been filed about medical personnel who walked into a waiting room where they discussed patients' HIV test results. Regardless of the outcome of the test, who wants to hear his/her HIV test discussed in a room full of other people?

Whether your information is contained in a physical document, in an electronic transmission, or given in conversation, it must be safeguarded. Those entities that are directly involved and any entities that have a relationship with them have to ensure they have a business associate agreement. This ensures the privacy rules are observed by all who interact with private information as part of doing business.

> **Whether your medical information is contained in a physical document, in an electronic transmission, or given in conversation, it must be safeguarded.**

Doctors' offices and pharmacies have sign-in sheets. Complaints have been made, and violations found, because some pharmacies left the sheets out where anybody could watch as patients signed in and wrote down medical information. Some of the sheets included protected health information (PHI).

The following table shows OCR's enforcement results by calendar year and type of closure. It includes the percentage of the total resolutions in each category.

Year	No violations found		Resolved after intake and review		Corrective action obtained		Total Resolutions
Partial Year 2003	79	5%	1177	78%	260	17%	1516
2004	360	7%	3406	71%	1033	22%	4799
2005	642	11%	3888	68%	1162	21%	5692
2006	897	14%	4128	62%	1574	24%	6599
2007	727	10%	5017	69%	1494	21%	7238
2008	1180	13%	5940	63%	2221	24%	9341
2009	1211	15%	4749	59%	2146	26%	8106
2010	1529	17%	4951	54%	2709	29%	9189
2011	1302	16%	4466	53%	2595	31%	8363
2012	979	10%	5068	54%	3361	36%	9408
2013	993	7%	9837	69%	3470	24%	14300

Image source: http://www.hhs.gov/ocr/privacy/hipaa/enforcement/data/historicalnumbers.html

HOW CAN MEDICAL RECORDS INFLUENCE A BACKGROUND CHECK?

Most of what my company, Sentinel, does is related to criminal records, SS traces, credit ratings, and DMV records. Medical information may be involved when we handle drug screening. Another rarity is information mentioned in a court record where it was part of the proceedings, such as a medical condition that has a bearing on the proceedings of the case to justify behavior. However, we think of it as our responsibility to be aware of all the HIPAA rules and comply with them. We take responsibility for the way we handle information and allow access to that information only to the people who have a legitimate right to it. We make sure job applicants have consented to share their information, and we facilitate patients' and job applicants' access to their report. This is part of being proactive and anticipating the needs and rights of all consumers.

In the case of drug screening, we facilitate the process by carefully selecting a responsible drug screener or lab, and we communicate with an officer trained in HIPAA. Typical handling protocol for test results involves sending samples from the lab to the medical review officer (MRO) and then directly to the employer. It's important to educate all parties involved.

The general principles apply here as well when it comes to securing consent, safeguarding information, using only relevant portions of the gathered information, using appropriate disclosure, and conducting proper disposal of information.

CONTROLLING YOUR MEDICAL RECORDS

As we go through life, we often acquire long medical histories. There are rules, regulations, and retention requirements pertaining to documentation.

Patients can be proactive and get copies of their records so they know what's going on, but copies may be maintained at different facilities, including doctors' and dentists' offices. There is no one central place where medical history is stored. That's what makes the United States different from, for example, some places in Europe, where there is one central holding place you can access to find out what's going on with your information. In the United States, information is held all over the place. You can never be 100 percent sure that all your information is being safeguarded in one place.

There are all these different laws, rules, and regulations, including federal laws, state laws, and industry specific laws. They sometimes intersect, creating a bunch of gray areas. Unfortunately, there is not one magic bullet to address this problem, but for now, what you can do is search the files and review the status of your own personal information.

The best way to do this is to be proactive in the interactions you have with physicians' offices. Review their policies and make sure the practices are reputable. Are they applying the right safeguards and appropriate measures? Most times, the onus falls on you to keep track of where your information may be stored. If you are concerned, contact that entity. The staff there can see what's going on with your information if they're still holding it and what's going to happen to it.

WHY IS IT HARD FOR PATIENTS TO ACCESS THEIR INFORMATION?

You'll notice that when you go to your doctor's office these days, there are more forms to fill out, and they're being updated more frequently. Among them is the opt-in or opt-out form that applies to information to be shared or provided. Usually, if the patient approves of the opt-in option, the benefit, or onus, falls a little bit more on the information gatherer. Health-care entities don't like these options much because they make it easier for patients to refuse to opt in. This means if patients don't check the opt-in box on the form, by default, they are afforded a little more protection from the sharing of nonmandatory information. The opt-out option makes a little bit more work for the patient, and the onus is on patients who later want to opt out. For instance, some health-care providers will ask patients whether they want to share health information anonymously with research partners or pharmaceutical companies. If patients don't opt out, by default, they agree to share their information with other entities. This step can be as simple as checking a box, or it can be a little more complex in that patients have to write and request to opt out or take other additional steps.

On the other hand, health-care providers need easy access to relevant information to expedite treatment or diagnosis. If a patient needs emergency care, nurses and doctors need access to the patient's medical history or medications, but they can't get access when the patient isn't able to provide permission. It gets tricky because restrictions shouldn't be so stringent they cause harm. Extremely complicated set-ups can hurt the patient. Awareness and training are useful for everyone from health-care providers and HIPAA-covered entities to patients/consumers.

There are numerous safeguards and rules, but there are loopholes. Corporate and public entities have to adhere to ethical standards. You, as a patient and a consumer, have to be educated, know your rights, read what you are filling out, know what's required information and what's going to be done with it, and know what's optional information.

Refusing to give patients access to their records can be a violation—for example, a doctor refusing to give patients access to their records because they hadn't paid all their medical fees. That's a violation of HIPAA. However, most of the time, a claimant can get some kind of resolution. The amount of effort will vary according to each particular situation.

If you're really adamant about getting your information, you may have to take several steps to get it. It could be as simple as submitting a written request. It may be as complex as obtaining a court order. It depends on what you want to do and how much you want to do it.

If you're really adamant about getting your information, you may have to take several steps to get it. It depends on what you want to do and how much you want to do it.

The OCR tries to protect consumers from situations like that and also from discrimination. The agency explains civil rights, health information privacy rules, and patient safety and confidentiality laws. It investigates complaints, so it's one of the places you can take your complaint if you think you are not being given access to something you have a right to access. You have to secure the consent of the person whose data you want to review, and you have to be clear about disclosures, what you're doing with the information, and the options available to that individual.

Personal data reviewers must be familiar with privacy standards and train, train, train. They are responsible for training their staff because even when everything is covered in writing, untrained staff may still divulge protected information in a public place or share it with the media.

You have to secure the appropriate contracts and agreements with any of your vendors who may come into contact with that information. You must secure their commitment. You have to be clear about what's optional and what's required. What's required can enhance quality of care or be used for research benefits. This also applies to genetic information, which is also protected.

CHAPTER 5

IDENTITY THEFT

Should we be worried about identity theft?

According to testimony from a deputy assistant attorney general in the US Department of Justice's Criminal Division, identity theft was the fastest growing crime in 2008, victimizing more than 10 million Americans.[6]

In the background check industry you can encounter identity theft in a couple of different ways. Employers are concerned about accidentally hiring a potential identity thief, who can gain access to people's personal information and therefore misuse it. Crimes committed by an identity thief can harm the victim of that identity theft even further, which is another cause for concern.

Big data is big business right now. Data is money. It is being compiled in all forms: graphics, written texts, and verbal communication. It is tracked and recorded from birth, and identifiers such as SS numbers are attached to it.

---

6 | "The Department of Justice's Efforts to Combat Identity Theft," US Department of Justice, Office of the Inspector General, Audit Division, March 2010, http://www.justice.gov/oig/reports/plus/a1021.pdf

As we progress through life, we build more and more personal data. We consume. We buy things. We acquire more official documents. We always have to wonder who is compiling that data and what they are doing with it, what controls are in place, and why. We must ask ourselves whether we gave the data up voluntarily or unknowingly by not reading the fine print. This happens a lot. People don't read the fine print. We frequently exchange our data for perks: coupons, discounts, and so on. Anytime we get something free, we're giving up data. Every time we throw a business card into a bowl, we're giving up our information.

All this data is being aggregated, sliced, and diced in many different ways. It's being packaged and sold, sometimes for legally permissible purposes and sometimes, unfortunately, for illegal purposes.

We have searchable identities that are used more and more to make decisions on whether to employ us, do business with us, go on a date with us, or market to us.

MANY PEOPLE HAVE ACCESS TO YOUR INFORMATION

When information comes from so many sources, it only makes sense to at least verify, or monitor, what information of ours may have been published. Extremes can range from information any average computer user can uncover to buried information that may only be uncovered by savvy private investigators, hobbyists, or malicious entities.

There are so many people with access (legal or otherwise) to your data it can be daunting. Much of the access to that data is justified. For example, when you sign up for a bank account, you have to give up that information because it's required by government regulations such as the Patriot Act, and know-your-customer (KYC) standards, with which the banks need to comply. There is usually a good intent behind access that is required—for example, to prevent money laundering or the hiding of criminal receipts and assets or terrorist financing. The Patriot Act was enacted to legalize such actions, including allowing banks to intensify their investigations of questionable activities.

In the past, if you wanted to look somebody up, you'd have to read a physical telephone directory to find someone's telephone number, and if a number wasn't published ... good luck. Within a couple of decades, all of that information is accessible via the Internet. In seconds, you can pull it up. Consumers themselves contribute to this ease of access because of all the data they give up voluntarily.

The evolution of technology, its speed, and the low cost of data storage and cloud hosting allow anyone to compile a ton of data.

PROTECTING YOURSELF
AGAINST IDENTITY THEFT

Business owners, employees, and consumers in general need to be aware of principles that help with better protection, not just those governing the use of computers. They govern print mail and phone calls in addition to use of electronic devices, such as computers, tablets, cell phones, and wireless networks.

Make sure you have an antivirus, antispyware program to prevent "Trojans" from leaving your computer vulnerable. Check your programs. Have you installed the latest updates for whatever browser you're using? This will help make sure there are no Trojans. A Trojan is a program or virus that gets into your computer and hides in your programs or system and can become active at any time for the purpose of stealing, destroying, or otherwise harming your data. Also, when you're not using your computer, lock it, and shut it down. Do not leave your computer as a target for hackers.

Be sure you don't do your sensitive work through insecure networks. Someone could be watching what you're doing. There are devices hackers can use to piggyback on what you're doing or actually access what you're doing with a view into your computer through the network.

Similar safety practices are needed during phone conversations. If someone calls you, claiming to be from your bank, don't give out any information. Contact your bank yourself and let the bank staff know, and you will find out if the request was legitimate. You have to watch out for spoofing. Don't click on links you don't recognize or open attachments you are not expecting, even from contacts familiar to you.

Be cautious about accepting insurance coverage updates on the Internet, especially exclusions and disclaimers that could rule out a possible benefit that you may think you are paying for but that won't be available when you need it. For instance, if you are paying for identity theft protection and become a victim of identity theft as a result of clicking on a phishing scam e-mail, identity theft coverage might be withdrawn from your policy or might be excluded because it is deemed an act of terrorism, which your policy might not cover.[7]

Sometimes, there are overlaps with insurance coverage you receive when purchasing additional products, such as bank products or services or house insurance. You may already have the needed coverage with the first product/service you paid for and not need to pay for the service twice.

Will they help you if you lose your wallet? Protection against lost wallets is important, as is the ability to freeze your personal reports or take the necessary actions to protect or retrieve your information. You always have to be aware of what information is being monitored. Is just your name and SS number being monitored, or are other accounts and public record filings being monitored?

> **Protection against lost wallets is important, as is the ability to freeze your personal reports or take the necessary actions to protect or retrieve your information.**

You also might need to consider monitoring your children's identity security, because they are issued SS numbers when they are born. When children are very young, they do not engage in financial activities, so it is easy to ignore potential problems.

7 | "Don't get taken guarding your ID," ConsumerReports.org, January 2013, http://www.consumerreports.org/cro/magazine/2013/01/don-t-get-taken-guarding-your-id/index.htm

Monitoring your children's identity security requires no more than general access to reports and scores and monitoring medical records.

Identity theft doesn't happen often, but when it does happen, it is scary. If you pay for a service, you have to make sure you have access to customer support and the knowledge base and are able to get your questions answered. You can also do it by yourself for free if you have the discipline to monitor your accounts online and scrutinize your credit reports. To do this, you can obtain three free credit reports at the same time, or you can obtain them at different times. For example, you could request a report from the first of the three main reporting agencies at the beginning of the year. You could get another report midyear from the second major credit reporting agency and a third one from the remaining major credit reporting agency before the end of the year.

You always have access to a free report if you are denied credit. You are supposed to be notified of the denial and which reporting agency's information was used to reach a decision. To clarify your credit status, you need the information contained in the rejection letter you receive. Contact that reporting agency to review your data.

INSURANCE

There are additional protections, either state protections or federal consumer protections. You may have insurance that covers some potential mishaps. Just be educated, aware, and proactive. There are resources you can refer to online, such as the FTC guidelines. Prevention is the best medicine.

At home as well, you have to be as cautious as you would be with electronic information. You should not write private details on paper and leave them lying out or share private information on the phone in a public place. While the party on the other end may be legitimate—for example, you may be talking to your bank—you may be providing your SS number so loudly others may hear it.

We'll rewind a bit to discuss the enactment of a law that helped bring awareness to these conflicts. There was a notorious case in 1998, involving an ID theft case. An ex-convict stole people's identities, bought a home, vehicles, and firearms, and even bragged about it. At that time, there were no specific laws addressing identity theft.

In the end, there was no restitution to the victim, who had to assume all the expenses of fixing the damage, restoring his/her identity, and clearing his/her names. The conman was finally arrested when he bought a firearm. He was charged with using a false claim to obtain the firearm. He ended up serving only a brief sentence, prompting a strong reaction from Congress, which enacted a law to define identity theft and make it a specific crime.

If you're traveling, have your post office hold your mail because criminals can get it, including your bills, IRS notifications, or other documents that may contain personal information allowing them to steal your identity. If you're suddenly not receiving your bills or if you get notices that changes to your address were made when you didn't, in fact, make those changes, there is cause for alarm. In this situation, you should notify all your creditors and other affected entities.

WHAT YOU CAN DO TO STOP IDENTITY THEFT

If you're a victim, you can call your local police. Make sure you get a police report and notify all your banks and financial institutions. You can contact your local FBI office. You can report the theft to the FTC, which has a consumer response center. It also has identity theft information and a checklist of steps to take, as does the US Secret Service, which also works on identity theft issues. The local postal inspection service also needs to be notified if your address was fraudulently changed.

If your SS number was compromised, you need to contact the Social Security Administration and also the Internal Revenue Service (IRS). Criminals may file taxes under your identity, or they may claim refunds. You may also want to check your state's consumer affairs department. Most states have departments that can provide appropriate guidance.

You have the ability to opt out of preapproved credit card and other offers that can lead to your name appearing on marketing lists. Ignoring such marketing ploys will reduce your chances of becoming a victim through the mail.

When you're talking to agencies, keep a log of specific details, such as whom you talked to and what you talked about. It may come in handy.

Criminals who steal your information can do anything you would be able to do yourself, except present themselves to friends and family who know you personally. Friends, and some members of your family, may even see your name being used, but if they're not entirely familiar with your personal information, they won't realize the use is fraudulent.

WHO ARE IDENTITY THIEVES?

Identity thieves may be criminals seeking financial gain. They may be people hiding from their own past, because they've committed crimes and need to take on the identity of someone who doesn't have a criminal record. They may be seeking a disguise in order to commit new crimes or terrorist activity. In some instances, identity thieves can be fugitives or illegal immigrants. These people might have been misled by gangs or cartels that operate an underground industry of smuggling illegals.

The IRS estimates that it erroneously paid $5.2 billion to identity thieves in 2013. The IRS said it identified and stopped short of paying another $24.2 billion. Still, those numbers may not be accurate; they could be much larger.[8]

How does this type of scam work? Criminals steal a worker's W-2 form from the mail and file a tax return using the W-2 owner's identity, gleaned from the SS numbers, name, and address on the form.

This works because the scammers file a request for a tax refund before the IRS has time to review the scam documents. Employers normally give their employees one copy of the W-2 and another copy to the IRS. They usually distribute employees' copies early in the year and send the IRS a copy later in the year for IRS staff to review and compare with tax returns. The IRS tries to issue refunds as soon as received and doesn't review refund claims immediately, sometimes not until midsummer, leaving a lot of time for errors to go overlooked. You can prevent W-2 theft

8 | "Additional Actions Could Help IRS Combat the Large, Evolving Threat of Refund Fraud," US Government Accountability Office, August 20, 2014, http://www.gao. gov/products/GAO-14-633?source=ra.

by having your W-2 delivered to a secure post office box if your employer has the option.

When thieves steal identities, they may have access to home ownership documents and the ability to change property titles. They may take out loans against homes that are not inhabited for a while or even sell them.

When thieves steal identities, they may have access to home ownership documents and the ability to change property titles. They may take out loans against homes that are not inhabited for a while or even sell them.

There was a case in one state in which a mentally unstable woman stole her daughter's identity. She wanted to roll back time, re-enroll in high school, and join the cheerleading squad, according to a local district filing.

In another case, a woman went into a hospital with a fake ID, delivered a baby, and walked out afterward, leaving the victim responsible for the bill. Hospital bills can amount to thousands of dollars.

Todd Davis, CEO of Life Lock, used to publish his SS number on his website. Davis became a victim himself in 2007, when his identity was used to take out loans and make purchases.

The movie, *Catch Me If You Can* is based on the life of a man named Frank Abagnale. He impersonated a doctor, a pilot, and other individuals. He cashed checks under different identities.

Be aware of these realities and monitor your information, your bank accounts, and your activity. Look for anything different or suspicious, such as failing to receive mail or bank statements. Safeguarding your information and your identity is mostly an issue of personal responsibility.

HYPOCRISY, ETHICS, AND CRIMINAL BACKGROUND CHECKS

Do you ever wonder what would happen if violators were caught for each violation they committed throughout their lives? Would we all have records? According to the National Employment Law Project (NELP), there are an estimated 65 million Americans with records. That's about a third of working adults. The records range from failure to pay a library or traffic fine to crimes of murder and rape. You cannot put all of these people in the same category and apply the same laws to all of them.

Some people will argue that background checks are unethical, but if background checks are unavailable, employers may fall back on their prejudices. They may assume that job applicants of certain races, ethnicities, or socioeconomic groups will be more likely to commit crimes and therefore avoid hiring applicants from groups against whom they harbor a strong negative bias.

You always have to ask, "Do people deserve a second chance?" What happens when you take away that hope of a second chance? Taking away opportunities, and the hope that accompanies them, leaves ex-convicts with no avenue to get back into mainstream life as good citizens. There are many states that deny convicted felons the right to vote, some of them temporarily, some permanently. In some places, such policies even extend to nonviolent offenders.

One should keep in mind the circumstances and severity of the crime, when it took place, and how the criminal has lived subsequently. We must infuse the human perspective into the process and not rely entirely on robots or application screening algorithms with yes and no answers or on incomplete information found on the Internet such as mug shots and arrest records that don't give the case dispositions. People can be accused and cases filed against them, but then later on, they may be found innocent.

Some employers see it as a trust issue. Once that trust is broken and a crime has been committed, trust may never be earned back. Some people say trust must be commensurate with the severity of the crime committed, the circumstances surrounding the crime. This makes a lot of sense, because not all crimes are equal, and there are, obviously, wrongful convictions.

Some states follow the three-strike rule, which may look very logical, but mistakes can happen with this rule. For example, individuals can have three minor violations that send them down that bad spiral. Some people go into the criminal justice system and to prison, and they come away as better people. Some come away as worse people.

Second chances should be earned. No one is entitled to anything, even a "first chance." Everything we do, we have to earn, so those looking for a second chance have to work a little bit harder to demonstrate they deserve it.

Wrongful convictions have been common throughout history. They include very serious crimes, such as murder. Many people on death row have been exonerated for crimes they did not commit.

Sometimes, decisions are difficult to make because of criminal laws that contradict each other. Be informed, be educated, be ethical, do the right thing.

In the background check industry, there are false positives as well as false negatives. A false positive usually happens when a crime is attributed to the wrong person because of an error in the process, and errors can happen at any point during the process.

Sometimes, decisions are difficult to make because of criminal laws that contradict each other. Be informed, be educated, be ethical, do the right thing.

There are ex-convict-friendly jobs and employers. You can search for those opportunities online by using the key words, "jobs friendly to felons." There are websites that list these employers.

Other things can affect an ex-con's ability to find work, such as the job market and current economy. The more choices employers have, the less likely they are to take on a convicted felon. Ultimately, ex-convicts must pick the right jobs to apply for, and sometimes, the competition is such that ex-convicts stand even less chance of getting the position they seek.

For both employers and ex-convicts, safeguards and precautions must be taken. Some state and federal laws ban ex-convicts from high-security jobs or work with vulnerable populations. Employers may have the worry of a negligent hiring lawsuit or workplace violence. Occasionally, employers find themselves stuck between a rock and a hard place. If they don't do a background check and something bad happens, depending on their state and jurisdiction, they are held liable. They have to worry about the EEOC coming after them for all sorts of possible violations.

Generally, between common sense and EEOC guidelines, employers must try to provide job opportunities to ex-convict applicants while simultaneously considering the nature of the crime, how long ago it happened, job qualifications, and the applicant's demeanor and attitude.

Some states offer incentives for hiring an ex-convict. Employers can sometimes get tax credits, and there are also federal bonding programs to help with liability and insurance. Some state and local workers' placement programs and career training programs try to encourage employers to hire people less likely to get a job by traditional means. Such programs provide motivation by offering employers a tax credit or free training for employees.

To put it all into perspective, some very successful, well-known companies were founded by people who used drugs, smoked pot, or had a criminal record. A lot of successful celebrities, musicians, and some of the actors people call the A-listers have overcome criminal pasts. This happens across all walks of life, but the repercussions hit some people harder than others.

However, while the founders of some successful companies have criminal records, they may not take their own experience into consideration when interviewing job candidates.

The EEOC itself has been accused of hypocrisy numerous times. In one incident, the EEOC sued an employer for running credit checks, but it was found that the EEOC itself ran credit checks for pre-employment purposes. The EEOC was fined for violating the Fair Labor Standard Act. In 1982 a court in Tennessee found the EEOC guilty of reverse discrimination when it turned down qualified white candidates in favor of African American ones. The agency suffered procedural setbacks in a couple of cases in which it went after companies, including BMW and Dollar General, according to case files in the Maryland District Court.

Hypocrisy regarding shared data happens at many different levels of society. It can happen at the government level. It can happen at the corporate level. Sometimes, federal laws clash with state laws. Sometimes, EEOC regulations clash with state law, but it remains to be seen whether the EEOC will take legal action against some of these opposing states.

Texas recently passed a bill to protect employers willing to give high-risk job applicants, such as ex-convicts, a second chance. They approved limiting the liability of employers who hire these people by offering employers some protection against negligent hiring accusations.

State laws that hold employers responsible for harm to others are referred to as "tort laws." It will be interesting to see if other states, besides Texas, begin to amend their tort laws.

Do the right thing. Make sure you have the correct background check and hiring policy in place. Make sure your job descriptions make sense and your hiring practices are responsible and legal. Be objective in your decisions as to whether a certain applicant is qualified or not. Remain conscious of not allowing your prejudices to seep into your decision making. Be consistent and show fair treatment.

Other issues and currently evolving trends to watch are those I've already mentioned throughout this book, including the ban-the-box movement to prohibit employers from asking about convictions on the application for employment and legalization of marijuana for medical or recreational use. Will it boil down to responsible use, as is the case with alcohol? Will discussions about this be evaluated in terms of relevance to individual jobs, or will other factors and stigmas dominate our conversations?

Information is a powerful tool, and we can use it to benefit people or harm them. It is easy, when we are surrounded by so much information, to judge others for their choices or pasts, yet not hold ourselves to those same standards of behavior.

Speaking of hypocrisy, during Prohibition, when alcohol was banned for the average citizen, Congress maintained a wine cellar. Congressmen had a personal runner who would supply them with wine, champagne, and different types of alcohol.

Information is a powerful tool, and we can use it to benefit people or harm them. It is easy, when we are surrounded by so much information, to judge others for their choices or pasts, yet not hold ourselves to those same standards of behavior. This is true in both our personal lives, and unfortunately, sometimes on the regulatory level as well.

HANDLING IRRELEVANT INFORMATION

When responsible credit reporting agencies run background checks for an employer, they omit results that are not relevant to the employer's legitimate needs. Some of the information these agencies are not allowed to pass on to employers include out-of-date cases, dismissed cases, and unverified information.

Sometimes, employers may only receive details of convictions from the past seven years. Sometimes, employers are allowed to obtain details from 10- or 20-year-old convictions, depending on the type of job they are offering and whether the employee will be interacting with vulnerable populations such as the elderly and children or working with a financial institution, where they will have access to personal information.

The decisions of employers and influential individuals are frequently motivated by fear of legal repercussions if a poor choice is made. Large amounts of money are at stake in lawsuits, as well as professional reputations. Legal consequences are likely to occur if a business does background checks incorrectly or if a discrimination lawsuit is filed.

Business owners and employers have a responsibility to perform background checks and gather data in an ethical way. They must shoulder that burden, as there is no one particular agency that polices this continuously to ensure total fairness.

Both employers and employees must listen to their consciences. Ask yourself, as a person in a position to hire someone, how ethical are you about this whole thing? If you are applying for a job, how honest are you about how you represent yourself and how you may have lived your life in the past? In any kind of controversial practice, there are those who try to do the right thing but find themselves fighting a battle against those who are cutting corners or misrepresenting information.

In my professional experience, I have had to turn away clients who were unwilling to comply with FCRA rules and guidelines. Before I pass information to them, I want to make sure they have a legitimate purpose, need, and use for it. Companies collecting credit reports need to first go through an on-site inspection to make sure of compliance with the required information security rules. They need to make sure that the right safeguards are in place. Sometimes, an inspection is denied. This can happen with landlords or employers, because they are not willing to update their legal forms to be compliant with FCRA regulations.

Business owners and employers have a responsibility to perform background checks and gather data in an ethical way. They must shoulder that burden, as there is no one particular agency that polices this continuously to insure total fairness.

Responsible background check companies compete with Internet websites, where you pay on the spot for cheap information that is not FCRA compliant. This information can be outdated, or superficial, public information. Clients who do not want to follow FCRA guidelines might opt to buy inaccurate or outdated information from such websites. They are doing themselves an injustice but either don't understand or just don't care. Sometimes, they want to just go through the motions and cut corners. With bigger companies, it's easy to assume there's an HR department carefully reviewing and completing the process in an ethical way, but businesses vary greatly in the way they are structured.

Workers and job applicants should stay alert for employers who are not as diligent or honest as they should be. There have been cases in which scammers started companies specifically to commit fraud. Bernard L. Madoff Investment Securities LLC, for example, cost investors tens of billions of dollars in losses. The IRS publishes examples of general fraud investigations that you can find on its website, or you can simply query *"American Greed"* or watch the episodes.

> Some employers just perform the process incorrectly. They're playing Russian roulette with their own businesses, because they miss new cases, lack information, or make themselves vulnerable to lawsuits.

If employers do their own background checks, they don't always have access to all the tools that professional agencies use. By law, a consumer reporting agency has to take out the dismissed and expunged cases, as well as cases that were completed more than seven years earlier, with some exceptions. When employers do this by themselves, there is no middleman making sure they are not looking at irrelevant and outdated data. There is also no law prohibiting employers from looking at expunged and dismissed cases if they show up.

Some employers just perform the process incorrectly. They're playing Russian roulette with their own businesses, because they miss new cases, lack information, or make themselves vulnerable to lawsuits.

When you work in this business, day after day, you see that it is an evolving and rapidly changing world. Courts change their processes and procedures, states' laws change, federal laws change, and regulators periodically issue different rules and guidelines.

It is worth noting that regulators can be overzealous at times. In 2013 the EEOC accused Peoplemark, Inc., in Tennessee, of discrimination based on criminal background checks, although the company also hired people with criminal records. The EEOC pursued this case in Tennessee Circuit Court but lost. It had to pay Peoplemark's legal fees for filing a wrongful lawsuit, which cost it hundreds of thousands of dollars.

Another point worth mentioning is that too many regulations or overlapping ones can create confusion. If the law becomes difficult for you, as a consumer, to understand, it becomes difficult to enforce and difficult to navigate by the entities governed by these laws. It becomes a minefield rather than something that's supposed to help people.

It is our job to stay on top of it, to communicate, and to be in it together with our customers. We look at it like a friendship. A good friend will try to stop you if you're going in the wrong direction or at least warn you. We don't have a problem telling prospects or clients they are disobeying rules or making themselves vulnerable by using inappropriate hiring procedures.

As I mentioned earlier, before I became an employer, I was an employee. Before I deal with consumer information, I acknowledge that I too am a consumer. In my own company, I work hard to combat hypocrisy and stay true to ethical standards. If something is not good enough for my own personal information, then it's not good enough for my employees' information, my clients' information, or my clients' employees' information. It's not good enough for anyone in the community.

THE ETHICS OF OVERLOOKING
A QUESTIONABLE PAST

Transparency is a central issue in consumer reporting and in the influence background checks exert on the lives of workers. When the law is followed and employers are transparent, consumer reporting agencies are transparent and applicants are transparent, and we can assume that good choices will be made.

There are also disclosure agreements in which applicants are required by law to represent themselves honestly. There are also limits, set by the government, on how old a case must be before it can no longer be used.

These guidelines have been put in place, but who polices them? Serious breaches only come to light once something stressful, such as a lawsuit, results from them, which then pushes the issue into the public arena.

Ultimately, because no one agency inspects all industries consistently to see if rules are being followed and ethics upheld, the fear of punishment, damage to reputation, and economic loss from lawsuits are the biggest motivators for businesses to keep themselves in check.

The important thing is to have a moral compass and take an ethical stance. If you're a worker, decide how much you are willing to put up with. Go and look for a company that's known to do the right thing.

Hiring practices reveal a lot about the integrity of a company. You should check your own records to make sure there's no inaccurate information reported there. You may want to have a conversation with your employer. What does your employer do with regard to background checks? What is the company's policy? Whom does the company use to gather data, or does the company gather it itself? Does the company use a researcher who's up to date with the industry standards and tries to do the best thing?

The National Association of Professional Background Screeners (NAPBS) was founded to establish standards and promote education. Membership rallies around encouraging ethical management and distribution of personal data.

However, there are still plenty of people who remain unaffiliated with organizations like NAPBS, who continue to operate on the periphery, performing questionable background checks and buying and selling data via obscure websites. In addition to those websites, there are different types of investigators providing a variety of reports. They may not be governed by the rules and regulations set forth by the EEOC or the FTC.

The following chart shows a typical EEOC process for handling complaints.

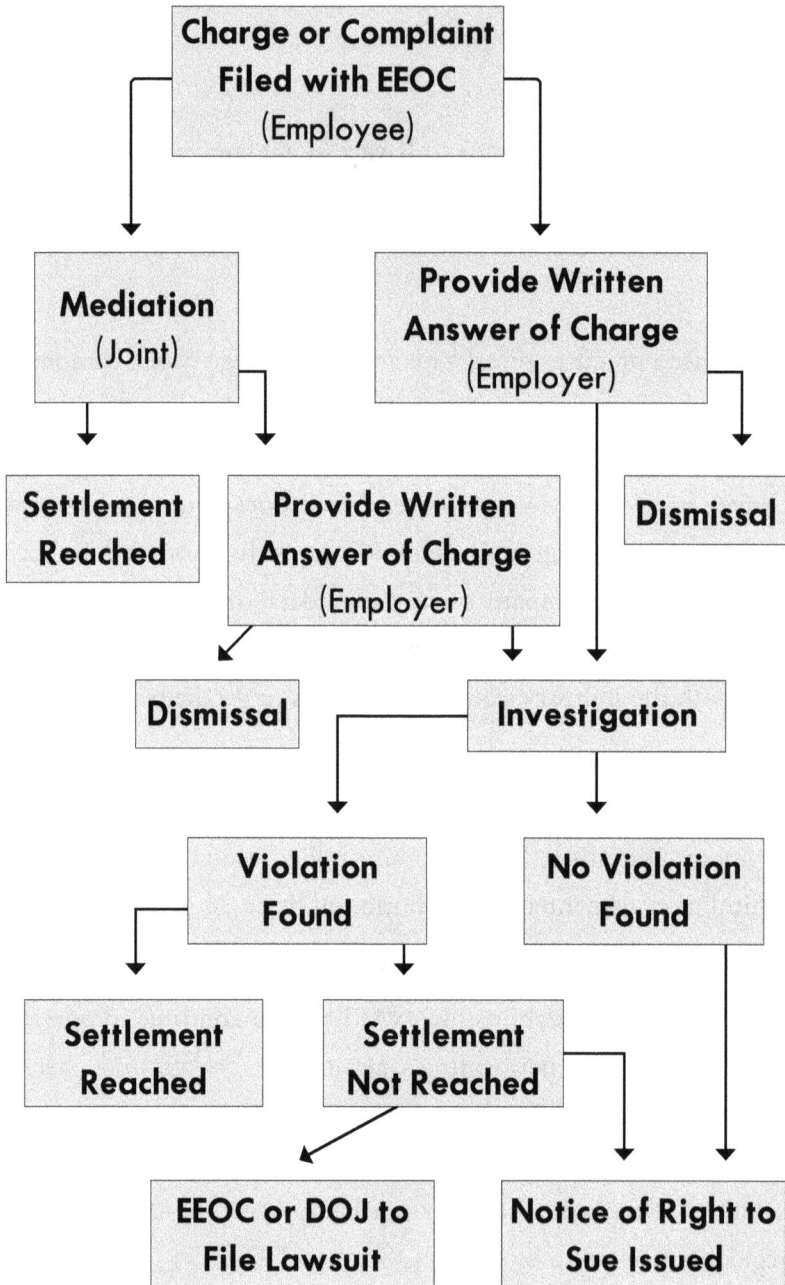

```
                    ┌─────────────────────┐
                    │  Charge or Complaint │
                    │   Filed with EEOC    │
                    │     (Employee)       │
                    └─────────────────────┘
            ┌─────────────────┴─────────────────┐
            ▼                                     ▼
    ┌───────────────┐              ┌─────────────────────┐
    │   Mediation   │              │  Provide Written     │
    │    (Joint)    │              │  Answer of Charge    │
    │               │              │     (Employer)       │
    └───────────────┘              └─────────────────────┘
      ┌─────┴─────┐                    ┌──────┴──────┐
      ▼           ▼                    ▼             ▼
┌──────────┐ ┌─────────────┐   ┌─────────────┐ ┌──────────┐
│Settlement│ │  Provide    │   │Investigation│ │Dismissal │
│ Reached  │ │  Written    │   └─────────────┘ └──────────┘
└──────────┘ │ Answer of   │
             │  Charge     │
             │ (Employer)  │
             └─────────────┘
```

Charge or Complaint Filed with EEOC (Employee)

Mediation (Joint)

Provide Written Answer of Charge (Employer)

Settlement Reached

Provide Written Answer of Charge (Employer)

Dismissal

Dismissal

Investigation

Violation Found

No Violation Found

Settlement Reached

Settlement Not Reached

EEOC or DOJ to File Lawsuit

Notice of Right to Sue Issued

DISPUTING BACKGROUND CHECKS

The goal of every responsible background check company or CRA is to make sure that information is accurate and verified. If we get inaccurate information from the court, for example, and share it with the applicant, the applicant may need to get the court to correct it.

If they can prove it, applicants can dispute erroneous data: "Okay. This could never be me, because I never lived at this address." "This is not my driver's license." "Even though this document has my name and date of birth on it, I was out of the country, and I can prove it."

Employers must look at all the details. They must dig deeper. Consumer Reporting Agencies prepare the reports, but ultimately, the employer, or landlord, makes the decision. It's their responsibility to say, "Okay. We've gone through the investigation, and the applicant has proven that the report refers to someone else. Here is the data. Here is the information."

IN THE DARK ABOUT YOUR DATA

When personal information is withheld from individuals, they're in the dark. They don't know what's going on. If inaccurate information is being circulated, they will never know and won't have a chance to correct it. They will continue to be denied opportunities, whether applying for work, insurance, a loan, or any kind of benefit.

Unfortunately, court records are available to the public, and sometimes, the courts sell them to different data brokers. Sometimes, voter registration information is gathered. Sometimes, gun owners' registrations and property records are shared publicly, and some sheriff's offices and prison systems publish personal information online. Some of them sell it to buyers who aggregate it, slice and dice it, and then distribute it. Some of these buyers are data brokers who split it into different products that they sell to a variety of buyers. Even the US Post Office sells information.

There are numerous buyers and sellers in the information industry. All you have to do is search online for your name, and you'll find data brokers wanting to sell you personal information— addresses, phone numbers, court records. It's a mish mash of different data, gleaned freely from sheriffs' offices, county jails, state prisons, federal records, and other law enforcement systems that make data available to anybody. Many people sell such information and sometimes, mismarket it to the wrong people.

Maybe one day, one legal entity will rein it all in and the government will make it illegal to gather personal data without the right qualifications and certifications and proof of legitimate use.

CHAPTER 7

DO THE RIGHT THING: NO EXCUSES

nformation can be attributed to the wrong person causing the denial of opportunities for jobs, loans, insurance, and other hardships or the ruin of a reputation. Incorrectly attributed information can jeopardize personal safety if published where the public can access it.

There is no flawless system, and there are no perfect people, so errors will happen.

PERSONAL INFORMATION IS NOT A COMMODITY

Responsible Background Check companies don't just retrieve personal records. When it is difficult to match a person to a record because of a lack of identifiers, we send someone to court to request the file, and we try to look for other attributes or identifiers that may match an individual with a record or prove the record does not refer to them.

We have had to even go beyond the federal records because, sometimes, their information may be incomplete. We have to do deeper due diligence and cross-referencing. We've had to get in contact with the district prosecutor's office in order to find additional information to figure out if the applicant was the one who committed the crime or if someone else with the same name—or even the same date of birth—was the real criminal.

We cannot get this from a data broker, because we are likely to end up with unreliable information. There is no one place where we can go and fix all of this at once. There is not one good place where we can have, for instance, criminal records checked. That's not something a broker can just sell for pennies. To do this correctly, experts must be involved. You have to have the right policies in place when you hire people. The more work you do up front, the less work you have to do in vetting, screening, and qualifying your hires.

The National Criminal Information Center is maintained by the FBI, and only the FBI, some law enforcement agencies, and entities with a special authorization have access to it. Special authorization is granted to individuals working with the government on projects requiring high security clearance.

When you deal with these issues, you need experts on different jurisdictions and different systems: how information is classified, how information is listed, how it is researched, what the shortcomings of that system are in each jurisdiction. You need a local expert who knows exactly when it is necessary to dig into microfiche or files or go to archives to get relevant information.

Anyone responsible for any part of this process has to be familiar with best practices. A researcher or records retriever must start with a general search and then narrow it down to get results that are relevant. This applies to public access terminals at the courts and many other search or inquiry systems. For example, if you are looking for someone named Michael Smith, you may search "Michael" or "Mike". There is an opportunity for a misspelling, so you may start with "Mi-" in what we call a search string or search extension. This tells the system to bring up everything that has M-I in it, regardless of whether it's spelled as Michael with a K or with a C, and then you search Smith. From there, you use other things to narrow down your search, such as date of birth, or address, or middle name.

People should know the difference between the filing of a lawsuit and a lawsuit that resulted in a judgment against the subject of your search. Anybody can sue anybody. Anybody can bring a lawsuit. Should you use a lawsuit just because it was filed? You need to look at the judgment and all the specifics before you make your decision.

With many screening products, you have to be aware of their best uses and limitations, how the information can be interpreted or misinterpreted, and what sources they use.

With many screening products, you have to be aware of their best uses and limitations, how the information can be interpreted or misinterpreted, and what sources they use.

Some products only become relevant when a job requires them. Security clearances are different. Different rules apply to drivers. Different rules apply in health care including licensing. The ethical stance is to gather only data that is relevant to the job.

Transfers of clearances, such as security clearances from one job to the next go through a special security officer. If they are not required, the special security officer cannot give you that information and can only verify limited information with the consent of the job applicant.

We're Concerned Consumer Reporting Agencies

If a company has been fined by the government for violation of rules, the violation will be published. Background check companies can be sued for not providing disclosures or failing to correct information in databases.

At Sentinel, we don't maintain a database. We always go to the source and get the most up-to-date information. Some companies maintain databases and add to them as they do business.

Usually, unethical operation of the database and convictions of violations following complaints are the reasons for some background check companies attracting news coverage. Some attract more news coverage than others do, depending on the size or gravity of the situation. A government agency may announce that a certain background check company was fined or a lawsuit played out in a court and became public record. The court's ruling will attract media coverage as well.

Your best bet if you want to research a background check company is to look at the National Association of Professional

Background Screeners. Its members are people who are committed to comply with the ethics and standards, the rules and regulations.

We at Sentinel are members of a group of companies called Concerned CRAs. That means Concerned Consumer Reporting Agencies. We all agree on one thing: responsible management and use of personal information, responsible dissemination, no outsourcing overseas or anywhere that would put the information in jeopardy.

One of the effects I hope this book has is to encourage background check companies, or any other entities we've been talking about, to realize that it is in their interest to do the right thing.

One of the effects I hope this book has is to encourage background check companies, or any other entities we've been talking about, to realize that it is in their interest to do the right thing. Don't just wait for an enforcer to come along and tell you or for a lawsuit to make it happen for you.

My book contains a lot of common sense and a lot of practices that center on being responsible with information retrieval, how you keep it and how you dispose of it, how you share it with only people who have a legitimate purpose, how you share it with the right permission, and how you don't do things behind the consumer's back.

REMEMBER THOSE WHO WERE NEVER CAUGHT BEFORE YOU JUDGE OTHERS

People can steal, and they can be dishonest in many ways, and sometimes, they are never caught for it and never have to answer for it. What happens to these people?

Offenders who are caught and learn their lesson can be more mature than those who have never been caught for criminal behavior and never had to face the consequences. Keep in mind that rejection can lead people in different directions. Sometimes, it leads people to being more creative, and sometimes it leads them to being destructive.

Some artists say they were inspired by a rejection for some reason or other. There are criminals who can say they resorted to being destructive because of some kind of rejection. Rejection, especially when it is unfair and repetitive, can spell destruction for a lot of people.

We all have to think of our role. We have to think about prison reform and rehabilitation. Lewis E. Lawes was an author, a warden of Sing Sing for 21 years, and an advocate for prison reform. We need to counter what he called "the passion and the prejudice aroused by crime." We need programs to teach compassion. We need programs that rehabilitate, not programs that breed more aggression.

WHERE DOES SELF-REGULATION COME FROM?

In my industry, our CRA policies and code of ethics are what brings everything together. They're drawn from our experiences. They're drawn from adhering to the rules and best practices of all the professional organizations of which we are members

The National Association of Professional Background Screeners, the National Public Records Retriever Network, Concerned CRAs, and all these agencies that we come in contact with influence our ethics and practices.

Principles in this industry come from information, from the FCRA rules and regulations, and the EEOC and HIPAA are taken into account, and, as I mentioned throughout the book, they all intersect at certain points.

We have people with law enforcement backgrounds. We have people who have worked in the banking industry. We have people who have done different types of investigations, are familiar and trained in information security processes, protocols, and in different codes of ethics.

We shore it all up with our code of ethics and our own internal policies that draw from all of these different sources. We go above and beyond by making sure we do the right thing, especially when we see there may be a gray area or a loophole. We know we will pass the test if our practices were ever put under scrutiny. We always operate under that premise.

CONCLUSION

MY MESSAGE TO YOU

I know the value of working hard to achieve something and wanting to safeguard it. I come from very humble beginnings, a rural area in Morocco where electricity and running water were scarce. I have empathy, and I have a sense of justice. I know the significance of working hard to achieve your goals. I always keep that in mind.

I grew up in a remote part of Morocco, which is what a lot of people would call a third world country. I grew up dreaming of having all these nice things, such as a particular jacket or a pair of tennis shoes that I couldn't afford. I was happy, though. I was able to eat, and I was able to drink water to survive. I wasn't starving, but I didn't have any luxuries, and I wasn't spoiled.

As a kid, I sold candy to the other kids. I would come into a small amount of cash, and I'd go buy a bag of candy, break it up, and start selling it piece by piece. As I got a bit older, I started raising bunnies and selling them. I saw a lot of things in my life as I was growing up, and I've lost a couple of friends too. In my late teens, I lost one to a motorcycle accident and another one, early on in the United States, to an overdose and didn't even know of any of his drug use before that. My life is full of all kinds of experiences.

> I always had a belief in myself in spite of all the odds. My experiences have left me with a sense of responsibility and opened my eyes to a lot of things.

It's been a life full of progress. I always wanted to do better. I always knew that I was going to give it my best shot and achieve. I always had a belief in myself in spite of all the odds. My experiences have left me with a sense of responsibility and opened my eyes to a lot of things. I know life is not always easy. It takes strength of character. It takes self-awareness and accountability to make it through. I know what different people go through at different stages of their lives. It is our duty to guide and mentor those not fortunate enough to have grown up with that such help.

I never like being taken advantage of or seeing other people get taken advantage of. Successful business people have often gone through hell to get to that point, and you must understand that they have to take certain precautions to keep their dream alive. We all deserve a chance to live our dreams.

HOW MY EARLY LIFE INFLUENCED MY PROFESSIONALISM AND WORLDVIEW

My background includes different types of work, from restaurants, hospitality, and banking to money laundering investigations to leading a team of analysts to great achievements and awards at a big banking institution.

I know what it is to be poor and be deprived. I know how easy it is to make a mistake. I also have a sense of personal responsibility, and I believe that working hard gets you somewhere.

Doing the right thing takes you far. I came back into the United States in 1993 and borrowed money to buy the air ticket. I started my life here with $400 borrowed in Morocco. That's what I came here with. The rest I just made happen for myself by working any place.

I went back to school to get my business degree. I took as many classes as fast as I could because I was impatient. I paid for school with a combination of working two jobs and taking out a student loan. For a couple of years, there was barely time to do anything other than work, go to class, and do homework. And none of that guaranteed anything.

When I was studying for the business degree, I had the option of picking a couple of different electives, so I chose criminal justice and psychology. I've always been interested in criminal justice, sociology, psychology, and how society works, how we all play a part in it, and how we can help each other.

When I left the hospitality industry, I was a manager trying to make the transition into another business. I had to take an entry-level job at Bank of America as a teller. From there, I started developing business skills.

In banking, I saw the consumer side of things as well as the business side of things. I saw who would come in with big deposits. I saw people being successful with their businesses. I also saw people struggling with overdrawn accounts, fees, and the vicious cycle that develops when accounts are overdrawn. I also saw how people get into trouble when they don't really understand how things work.

THE COMMITMENT I BROUGHT TO SENTINEL

The business started initially as a bootstrap enterprise. I co-founded it and ended up acquiring the other shares within the first couple of years. I started working out of the house, and from there, I went on to have multiple employees. We went from infancy in 2007 to being named one of the Fast 50 by the *Tampa Bay Business Journal* in 2012 and coming in number 7 out of the top 50 fastest growing companies in the Tampa Bay area based on percentage of growth.

We have 12 direct employees, and we are growing, and we work with hundreds of carefully selected and vetted independent contractors who retrieve court information for us in other states. We leverage technology and expertise because there is so much available now. We integrate with our customers a lot, so we eliminate a lot of the errors that come from manually inputting data from one computer to the other.

We don't gather information to sell it. We don't keep records. We're not an information broker. We go to the courts to get the information. We go to the source. We rarely use databases and don't recommend to employers that they only use databases. They can use them as a supplement to point them in certain directions, but they still have to validate that information. We don't maintain a database ourselves, and when we need the services of a database provider, we most definitely select only one or two that have demonstrated they take the appropriate measure to verify as much information as possible, but we still don't just take their word for it. We still verify it ourselves.

We are more than just a data provider; we deliver a variety of customized background and tenant screening services. We usually do this by talking to the customers about their specific needs because one size does not fit all.

Our company employs people who have gone through law enforcement training, served as drug enforcement agents in the US Drug Enforcement Administration (DEA), or are former military. We have people who have done background checks for decades. Together they bring both investigative and risk management experience.

We have a diverse, multigenerational team. Our people come in with the right values and embody our culture, and we put them through a rigorous training. They learn about the industry, how it works, about our values and our ethics, and how we conduct business.

We bring it all together around our values and our culture, which centers on integrity and service. Everybody we hire has to fit into this culture. We are strategic in our decisions concerning our customers, employees, and our community, and we understand the value of trust.

We love what we do and see value in the services we provide to our clients. We exercise versatility and flexibility in working with our clients, providing additional options, training, or other assistance needed in order to help them uncover the right information.

Our team is committed to not only providing a service but to executing it correctly and efficiently. We pledge to communicate clearly and regularly. We believe our clients are the heart of our business and encourage them to communicate questions, concerns, or suggestions on a regular basis. We show and have empathy for our employees, our clients, our community, and consumers.

We commit to fostering an environment that is conducive to not only understanding but having a positive impact on those around us. Anyone who works with us has to believe and embody these qualities.

We commit to fostering an environment that is conducive to not only understanding but having a positive impact on those around us. Anyone who works with us has to believe and embody these qualities.

We have the right protocols and a secure system of electronic integration to transmit data to our customers. Our researchers log in securely from different places, whether Kentucky or Louisiana or Tennessee, to a secure web portal where they retrieve the search requests. Then, they go to court to get the requested information and input it back into our secure portal to review it. It goes through a quality review process, and the relevant information is passed on to the customer.

Visit our blog for updates and relevant case studies and related articles at www.sbchecks.com/blog or select the resources tab for more job applicant and employer resources.

WHY OUR CUSTOMERS LOVE US

We keep people at the center of everything we do. Unless they run a company staffed with robots, most organizations rely on their people to carry out their mission and vision. The better the selections they make, the more successful they are. If they get it wrong, they miss out on business opportunities or get into legal trouble or lose their business.

The Society for Human Resource Management conducted a survey that showed the biggest frustration among customers of background check companies was customer service, or rather, lack of customer service. When a different organization did the same survey with customers of background check companies and asked them what makes a company stand out, the majority said good customer service.

Don't take our word for it. You can go to our website and read customers' testimonials.

Our customers know that everybody has the technology and resources to move information around, but they want an expert on the other end of the phone who knows the industry, who can walk them through the necessary steps and explain the terminology and the process.

It has to be someone who's in it for the long haul with them, someone who takes their reputation seriously, not just a fly-by-night operator looking to make a quick buck, regardless of what damage is left in the aftermath.

Some of our customers worked with other companies, which they left because they were not able to get their calls returned or call and get a real person on the other end of the line. They were treated like a number and sent invoices, but they were not getting their questions answered.

They were sent to different automated systems, routed to websites to sift through information, forced to figure things out on their own. We talk to you throughout the process, from beginning to end and beyond. That's what our customers like about us. What makes us different from other companies is that our customers have access to seasoned professionals. They can e-mail and call, but they always get that personal response. There's no automation when what's needed is human interaction. That's how we work. We take our reputation seriously and our customer service seriously, and we help our customers throughout the whole process. We are honest. We will not take just any type of business. If prospective customers don't agree to be responsible, go through the right steps, the vetting process, and demonstrate a legitimate need for information, the willingness to comply with regulations, and the willingness to change any processes or procedures that are inappropriate, we are upfront in letting those prospective customers know that we are not a good match for them.

Ask yourself if you have the right practices, the right policies, and the right procedures in place. Are you using the best resources and the most qualified vendors? Background checks are not a luxury. They are a necessity. Reach out to us by calling or contacting us through our website for a free, no-obligation consultation and review of your needs and your current policies and practices.

WE RESPECT OUR CUSTOMERS AND OUR COMMUNITY

We have agreements, but we don't lock customers into contracts as some of our competitors do. We don't have any membership or starter fees. We don't have minimum orders. We don't nickel and dime our customers. Our customers do business with us because of our excellent service, not because of contractual obligations.

You need to keep all of that in mind when selecting a vendor. Keep in mind that doing the right thing may not always come clearly and easily, but people will always know when you've done your best and when you've followed procedures and put in the effort to try and do the right thing.

You don't want to discriminate or deny people an opportunity for the wrong reasons. Sometimes, you are not ready for job applicants, and sometimes they are not ready for you. It's okay to say that, and people will respect you for it.

If you are a job applicant, appreciate the fact that the business owner has poured sweat, maybe life savings into that business, and if you are a business owner, understand that not everyone who applies for a job is out to get you. Think before you make a decision based on inaccurate or incomplete information and turn away someone who could be a great asset. Hiring the wrong person for the wrong reasons does an injustice to both employer and employee but so does not hiring the right person for the wrong reasons.

Keep all this in mind when you're making decisions in a position of influence. Good, reliable information is not a luxury; it's a necessity. This is something you shouldn't play Russian roulette with.

Make a commitment to your customers, yourself, your employees, your vendors, and your community to be as ethical as you can be with this great responsibility.

www.ingramcontent.com/pod-product-compliance
Lightning Source LLC
Chambersburg PA
CBHW050510210326
41521CB00011B/2400